Apostles

Apostles

A Candid Take on Managing Organisations and Talent

Biswaroop Mukherjee

Copyright © 2024 Biswaroop Mukherjee

Biswaroop Mukherjee has asserted his rights under the Indian Copyright Act to be identified as the author of this work.

All rights reserved under the copyright conventions. No part of this publication may be reproduced or transmitted in any form or by any means, electronic or mechanical, including photocopying, recording or any information storage or retrieval system, without the prior permission in writing from the publisher.

This book is solely the responsibility of the author(s) and the publisher has had no role in the creation of the content and does not have responsibility for anything defamatory or libellous or objectionable.

BluOne Ink Pvt. Ltd does not have any control over, or responsibility for, any third-party websites referred to in this book. All internet addresses given in this book were correct at the time of going to press. The author and publisher regret any inconvenience caused if addresses have changed or sites have ceased to exist, but can accept no responsibility for any such changes.

ISBN: 978-93-92209-90-1

First published in India 2024
This edition published 2024

BluOne Ink Pvt. Ltd
A-76, 2nd Floor, Sector 136, Noida
Uttar Pradesh 201301
www.bluone.ink
publisher@bluone.ink

Printed and bound in India at Nutech Print Services

Kali, Occam and BluPrint are all trademarks of BluOne Ink Pvt. Ltd.

Contents

1. Authentic Leadership — 1
2. Built to Change the Organisation of Future — 4
3. Can't Keep Calm? Practice Mindfulness — 8
4. Employee Experience Decoded — 11
5. High Performance Is All About Managing Behaviours — 14
6. How to Make Better Career Choices — 18
7. Leadership and Legacy — 22
8. Leading with Trust — 24
9. Meetings: A Contemporary Challenge at Workplace — 29
10. The Role of a Leader — 32
11. When Good Is Not Good Enough — 35
12. An Effective Leader amidst Crisis — 38
13. An Effective Way to Deal with Adversity — 41
14. Appreciative Enquiry Enables Collaborative Change — 44
15. Careers Are Marathons, Enjoy the Journey — 47
16. Fostering Innovation: Creating a Culture of Embracing Failure — 50
17. Creating a More Effective Learning: Interventions in Digital Mode — 53
18. Effective Performance Management System — 56
19. Crystal Gazing: Emerging Trends in HR — 60
20. Enable and Enforce: A Critical Balance for an Effective HR Leader — 63

21.	If Humans Are a Resource, Do We Account for Talent?	67
22.	It's Time We Rename HR	79
23.	Leadership Series: Decision-Making	82
24.	Learning Is Personal and Capability Development Is Organisational	84
25.	Managing Performance Is Not About Post-mortem; It Needs to Be Fed Forward	87
26.	Two Axiomatic Phrases towards Higher Organisation Effectiveness	90
27.	Performance Culture: What Is It All About and Did You Notice It?	93
28.	*Can Do* Is Potential, *Will Do* Is Succession and *Done It* Is Performance	96
29.	The Office Is Dead, Long Live the Office	100
30.	Three Simple Steps to Effective Talent-Development Strategy	104
31.	Tough Times Never Last but Tough People Do	107
32.	Why Did You Take HR?	109
33.	Attributes That Make a Leader	112

About the Author   115

ONE

Authentic Leadership

Authentic leadership is amongst the most researched topics today under the subject of leadership. This is surely one of the traits that really enables a leader to grow their area of influence and create a lasting impact in their line of work. The reason why it is being researched a lot is because we are still unsure of how to measure it and what exactly it should look like. We know if a leader is authentic or not, yet we are not too sure of the parameters or measures that make a leader authentic. We hope the jury will be out soon.

Let's understand why authenticity in leadership is so much in demand today. It's in demand because people want someone real, someone who doesn't say something to them and does something else. In the VUCA[1] world, paradigms are changing, life is day by day becoming more uncertain, so people want to be led by someone who is genuine, who is real, and who understands them as a person more than ever and can connect with them.

There are a lot of dilemmas around being authentic in the minds of many leaders as organisations by the definition

---

[1] Volatility, Uncertainty, Complexity, and Ambiguity

of it will have their political overtones and there will be ways of working around the political affiliations of an organisation. There is always the worry whether being authentic will create challenges for the leader amidst the political affiliations, which is the reason why a lot of leaders like to play the game as it's played at the place. Authentic leaders are well versed with the political overtones and are able to navigate the organisation with utmost sincerity, commitment, and transparency. The political overtones do not deter them from doing the right things for the greater good of the organisation. These leaders transcend regimes or groups of political affiliations in an organisation over a period of time and grow stronger within the organisation and create more authenticity for themselves as leaders in the process.

Here is my take on the traits of an authentic leader. Hope it will enable you to spot them and inspire you to be an authentic leader:

Authentic Leaders Lead with Their Hearts and Not Just Their Minds

They are not afraid to show their emotions, their vulnerability, and they also have a penchant for connecting with their teams at a personal level to enable them to lead better lives.

Authentic Leaders Do Not Shy Away from Having Difficult Conversations

They are able to provide direct feedback to their teams, and because of the level of authenticity, the team members take the feedback with utmost sincerity. This quality of authentic leaders enables them to turnaround people and work cultures with a lot more ease than it is for the others.

Authentic Leaders Refrain from Creating Affiliations for Any Reason

They don't play favourites. For them anyone who creates value for the organisation is the one to be revered irrespective of any personal likes or dislikes. This trait enables professional behaviour and approach within the team. The team realises, that it's their performance that matters and nothing else.

Authentic Leaders Think and Act Long Term

They are not short-sighted, and they never take a short cut. They create legacies and foundations for the organisations where they work. This long-term orientation enables them to create significant milestones along the way.

Authentic Leaders Are Transparent and Candid

They ensure that they are consistent and open about their thoughts and actions across levels. This helps to build trust in a team and any team is always ready to walk the extra mile for a leader they trust.

TWO

Built to Change the Organisation of Future

We are in an era today where mergers and acquisitions, industry consolidation, inorganic growth, cross-market joint ventures are a way of life and are the new normal. They are much more than ever before. It used to happen earlier too, in last few years, it has gained tremendous momentum. An employee joins an organisation owned by a specific group of shareholders of one country, and in a few months' time the shareholders of the organisation change to one of a different origin and country. In certain cases, even the brand name of the organisation changes. We are also witnessing the culture of serial entrepreneurs who are building businesses to sell and then move on to the next one. More importantly, there is no geographical borders for all these changes and transaction that are happening. Promoters are increasing revenues though incurring losses to gain more consumers to enable a better valuation eventually when they sell off the organisation, it's all happening in the marketplace today much more than ever before. Clearly the algorithms of doing business and making profits are shifting paradigms.

In such a changing world, the way we manage human resources has to be significantly different from the way we have been managing it so far. It is because of two reasons: the business demands a different approach, and also the employee mindset, especially of the millennials, is no longer the same.

Let's reflect on some of the tenets for managing human resource that need an overhaul to match the current and upcoming business requirements and context.

Hire for Agility and Ability to Deal with Ambiguity

It's not about the long list of competencies you hire for, they are not cast in stone anymore as the changes are much more rapid. Organisations need to hire and develop talent on being agile in learning the ropes and thus having the ability to change as the context demands. Another important competency organisations should hire for is the ability to deal with ambiguity as situations are highly likely to be a bit ambiguous as changes are more rapid in nature. A strong ability to deal with ambiguity will enable to deal with the unknown better and manage disruptions more effectively.

Compensate for Quick Wins and Load It Exponentially for Bigger Wins

The compensation structures, in a built-to-change environment, with less job security and high ambiguity need to ensure that the performers are continually compensated for quick wins and exponentially for larger wins, else the performers would move away to an organisation in which there is more permanence of jobs, less risks, and less ambiguity.

Organisation Effectiveness and Development Key Themes for HR Teams

A continuous focus on organisation's effectiveness and development has to be driven by HR teams to enable their organisations to handle all kinds of changes and disruptions in the marketplace effectively. Cost versus value, spans and layers, cultural implications, planning mechanisms, productivity mechanisms, etc., need to be constantly tracked and made even better all the time to remain competitive in marketplace.

An Open, Transparent, and Candid Culture

It's important to cut hierarchy and bureaucracy in an organisation which is built to change and promote a candid culture to enable the organisation to be fast paced in driving change and constantly being in touch with customer requirements that are key to growth. A lot of times customer connect and market understanding get compromised in a closed culture, and in a disruptive environment there is heavy penalty for reading the market late.

Curate a Network of Talent Both Internally and Externally

Talent works for roles and assignments and may not be ever after as it used to be. In a built-to-change scenarios it's important organisations have an understanding of the talent pool available both internally and externally, continually curate talent communities around it, and are quickly able to tap into the resources whenever there are talent requirements for the business—be it internally or externally. In a changing world with lot of options for employees as well in the marketplace, it's important that organisations curate network both internally and externally and not just internally through lengthy succession plans as it has been carried out traditionally.

THREE

Can't Keep Calm? Practice Mindfulness

As we transform towards digitally enabled organisations, digitally enabled workplaces, and digitally enabled smart homes and home appliances, the omnipresence of digital tools and network in our lives is a necessity to stay ahead and a must have to keep pace and stay connected with others—be it professionally and personally. If we reflect on how technology has changed our lives, it will be surprising to learn that only a decade back, we were so less digitally dependent; so much lesser was the influence of technology on our lives. Things which are an integral part of our world today were just another new fad happening yesterday in that space. With the advent of this digital revolution, we all have observed changes in our behaviour—both at workplace and at home. I remember, in organisations social media were banned over local area network, and employees using social media during office hours were looked at in a different way and at times reprimanded. Today, even the big boss is posting update on social media during office hours. Such is the change in our lives at workplace in less than a decade. We have teams managing social media for the organisations and posting regularly to build brands. At home, the scenario is not so different either. An internet breakdown has much more severe effect than yesteryear's electricity breakdown. Such is the digital influence in our lives.

Amidst all these transformations, I am sure each one of us have noticed the changes in our social and official etiquettes, we no longer switch off phones during important meetings, we keep chatting during meetings, we keep texting even when someone is talking to us in person both at work and home, we are so easily oblivious of our surroundings both at work or home, etc. How often have we been in a situation where there is a conference call, a WhatsApp chat and an mail to respond and often we are juggling between all these modes of communication; to top it all at times there is someone knocking at the desk for a quick decision and we participate in that as well while muting the conference call. This kind of incessant multitasking takes a toll on our mind without us knowing and thus becomes the biggest source of stress for individuals today. Bad multitasking which we are getting more used to creates higher stress levels, lower attention spans, and poor listening skills. It impacts the mind and body and the output all three eventually and at times it leads to psychosomatic disorders which are often unrepairable and only controllable. From an output perspective as well, there is adverse impact of bad multitasking due to our digitally enabled lives, as our attention span becomes lower, we are able to understand less, reflect less on the problem and thereby the solutions also are not holistic to the extent needed thus impacting the delivery outcomes. If both from health and wealth perspectives this digital multiplexing is bad for us, then what are the ways to get over the menace which is an omnipresent in our lives?

The easiest way to get out of the ill effects stated above is to practice mindfulness. There are programmes, trainings, books, and many more to aid each one of us in mindfulness, however for me mindfulness is simply being in the present and enjoy what we have around us at that moment. How many times we pass by a road and not even look at the beautiful building on the side of the road or the amazing tree which has got flowers of unique colours because things of past or future are going on in our minds, which are continuously being stoked by digital enablers in some way or the other. Mindfulness is about enjoying the present being aware of the surrounding, participating in the conversation that is happening now with both body and mind. As we practice of dealing with, appreciating, understanding or listening one thing at a time, as we be aware in mind and body of the here and now, we are being mindful. The mere self-discipline on this will create huge levels of de-stress due to being mindful. Habits like physical exercise, pursuing a passion around music, reading, photography anything which consumes us is a good way of being more mindful. To conclude, in this digital world the marketer is continuously looking to get more of your attention in the digital space of the product or service however it's important that each one of us are mindful of our mind.

FOUR

Employee Experience Decoded

As the war for talent intensifies and we witness the entry of Gen Z into our organisations in the years to come, one of the key tenets for prospective talent to choose one organisation over the other will be the experience. Experience is a very subjective term and is often not aptly defined, hence, it's difficult to understand employee experience and even more difficult to set up a road map for the organisation to create a best-in-class employee experience.

A great experience can only be provided if we are aware of the expectations of the talent from the organisation. Hence, it's important to understand their needs, desires, and feelings to really understand and meet expectations. To decode the employee experience, it's important to define the expectations to be addressed. Various sets of talents in the marketplace would have various expectations based on their own set of beliefs, motives, and values. Hence, it's important to align those expectations of experience decoded with the organisational values and then define the proposed employee experience framework. This alignment is important as the organisation would want to attract and retain talents that align with organisation's cultural priorities. Thus, to get the employee experience decoding right, it's important that user-centric design and employer branding are aligned with cultural priorities before defining the experience. The given diagram provides perspective on how to create the intended employee experience.

Across the year and through their career with an organisation, employees will go through various experiences. Hence, to create a great employee experience, it's important to look at all the touchpoints of the organisation with an employee across the life cycle. This is one of the reasons employee experience is seen as the next big thing in the HR domain, because it encapsulates the entire framework of HR across domains within HR.

To provide an amazing employee experience it's important to decipher each of the tenets of the HR function and then build the experience metrics across each of them and then institutionalise the process. Institutionalising employee experience thus is a mammoth task and requires years of perseverance for large organisations to set it right and further progress on the same. Every organisation today is grappling with building the employee experience story and looking at various models to enable them in the journey. I have put together a model which can enable organisations to understand employee experience and institutionalise it.

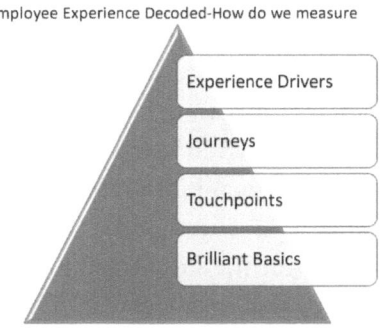

Employee Experience Decoded-How do we measure

The model as depicted in the diagram provides an overview of the architecture of development and measurement of employee experience. Hence, to build an employee experience framework, it's important to draw up experience drivers like talent, capability, onboarding, career growth, etc. On each of these experience drivers, employee journeys need to be created for the entire employee life cycle. Once that is done, we get the employee touchpoints in terms of where are the points in which employees are experiencing each of these experience drivers in their journeys. On each of these touch points it's important to create a robust process and system to enable a great experience every time the employee reaches the touch point, thus brilliant basics are to be created to enable the processes and systems which essentially is all about ensuring execution excellence in each of these dimensions.

While employee experience may seem to be a buzzword and evokes a feeling of next-level initiative in reality it starts with brilliant basics and operational experience of the basic HR processes. These basic HR processes of an organisation today are often outsourced and driven through shared services. To summarise, to get the employee experience right it's important to create the framework and back it up with exemplary execution excellence.

FIVE

High Performance Is All About Managing Behaviours

Organisations and businesses across the globe are being run with the objective of growing their bottom line. The more progressive ones are chasing triple bottom lines of social, environmental, and financial, and the lesser ones only financial. Irrespective of the level of progressiveness, it's thus all about achieving consistent growth in the bottom line for an organisation.

In a competitive global scenario amidst a VUCA world to achieve consistent growth requires a high level of precision in business strategy and execution excellence to action out the strategy. The precision in making strategy and delivering excellence in execution in an organisation both come only through its people. It's the people in the organisation which helps achieve the consistent growth in bottom line and makes an organisation stand out amongst its competitors and make it great.

What do people do in top-notch organisations that others don't, which make them the best in class? What are the behaviours that are demonstrated at workplace by people in the best organisations, which lead to the outcomes that are not there in the rest? To understand more of the behaviours demonstrated by people in best-in-class organisations, let's first understand what 'behaviour' means. Behaviour is defined as the range of actions and mannerisms made by individuals in conjunction with themselves or their environment, which includes the other systems or organisms around as well as the (inanimate) physical environment. It's important to note in the definition of behaviour three words are very important: actions, individuals, and environment. If we synthesise these three words, behaviour can simply mean individual action in a given environment. The behaviour of an individual in a given organisation is thus all about actions that an individual displays in the organisation.

Behaviour (Y) = F (action, individual, environment)

Let us reflect deeper into the levers of behaviour in the organisation that drive superior organisational outcomes.

- **X = Environment:** The environment in one organisation can be different from another organisation; this is due to organisational culture. Organisational culture encompasses behaviours that contribute to the unique social and psychological environment of a business. Thus, organisational culture affects the way people and groups interact with each other, with clients, and with stakeholders. Given that the environment in which the individual displays action varies due to the organisation culture, it is imminent that the demonstrated behaviours acceptable and applauded in one culture may not be acceptable in another culture. Thus, it's important to choose the values and behaviours carefully that create the organisational culture. In creating the organisation culture it's important to define the values which are essentially broad preference of behaviour disposition to reinforce the cultural priorities. Organisations both old and new should consistently review these cultural priorities called values basis the organisational context and the market context both of which are dynamic in nature. Processes and systems built for managing people should clearly reinforce these values all the time, and whenever there is a need to reinvent these values, it's important to change and redesign the people processes and systems so that the reinforcements of the cultural tenets are consistent with the new values of the organisation; hence, cultural change aligned with market requirement is an ongoing process and not a gigantic step to move from a fossilised outlook to a millennial outlook, which creates a lot of turbulence.

- **X = Individual:** The individual in an organisation displays behaviour based on knowledge, skills, and attitude. These attributes are based on the values, motives, beliefs, and traits of the individual. It is important to evaluate these attributes while hiring to enable a better cultural fit. For individuals already in the organisation, it is important to continuously educate, reinforce, and guide them to change their behaviours to the cultural tenets of the organisation. The role of leadership is paramount in making the change of behaviours continuously of individuals in an organisation as organisation culture is built not on what leaders say but what they do. Hence, it's important for leadership to walk the talk in terms of displaying behaviours that the organisation wants to drive in its employees towards building a certain culture in the organisation.

- **X = Actions:** To enable the individual to act in a certain manner in an organisation, it is important to provide the individual references of actions and thus drive the targeted behaviours. To enable the reference of actions, organisations create competencies, which are nothing but demonstrated behaviour descriptors, to drive actions that are targeted towards enabling behaviours aligned with their culture and strategy. Behavioural competencies are created basis the culture tenet, that is, values and functional competencies are created basis the business outcomes required functionally for each and every function. Organisations should have their set of behavioural competencies and functional competencies clearly defined to drive the actions they intend the employees to take for targeted behaviour outcome. It is also important to continuously change the competencies both behavioural and functional basis the market and organisation requirement.

In essence people in high-performing organisation display behaviours which are carefully crafted by the leadership of the organisation to enable the high performance as an outcome.

SIX

How to Make Better Career Choices

Whenever we look at changing our present job, be it inside the organisation or outside, the four clear things that come to our mind for evaluation of the new role are:
- The level of the new role in organisation hierarchy versus the current one
- The compensation and benefits associated with the new role versus the current one
- The span of the new role versus the current one
- The exposure the new role will provide us to our area of work

If the role is outside the organisation, then we additionally look at the organisation culture of the new organisation and brand reputation of the organisation in the market.

A successful career is a function of making the right career choices and balancing the same with both professional and personal aspirations. Once we evolve in our careers the aspirations become clearer, as we gain more professional expertise, understand how it works in organisations, we get more career options and choices with our skillset and competence, as our basic financial requirements are taken care. The more we evolve in our career, the more we are clear with the aspirations and a lot of times we reset the milestones for ourselves both in professional space and personal space we had set out in the beginning of our career while being students. As we evolve in the career journey the milestones become much clearer and the eagerness becomes more strong to achieve them for a perfect finish to our careers which we build with so much of hard work and sacrifices.

While making the career choices we often tend to lean towards the professional aspirations more, as we feel that personal aspiration is actually an outcome of the professional aspiration. If we grow and succeed in our professional aspiration, we can make our personal aspirations come true. This is the key assumption due to which we tend to evaluate any new role basis the criteria's mentioned above and not anything else. The challenge with such unidirectional evaluation criteria for career choices is that we often to tend to hit road blocks in this journey as we tend to understand ourselves more as we evolve in our careers and with career growth and affluence we tend to look at aspects like doing what we like, we tend look at our purpose for existence, we tend to look at personal aspirations related to giving back to society, we tend to look at spending more time with family, we tend to look at creating lasting imprints on the work we do and eventually build a legacy, we tend to look at providing more comfortable and secure life to our near and dear ones.

To avoid such roadblocks, it's important to have a high level of self-awareness and clear understanding of the context, content, and impediments of the industry and roles we want to get into. Unfortunately, at an early age, we have neither, and even if we think we do, in reality, we still do not. Also, most importantly in an ever-changing world with numerous disruptions, the entire context might have changed from what we set out to do and what we land up with after, say, 10 years. To ensure a better career decision, reflect on the aspects mentioned below and probably you will make better career decisions and land up with a great choice.

Understand Who You Are

Reflect on yourself. What kind of a person you are? What kind of personal aspirations you have? What are the traits you have as a person and what are your strengths and development areas? What is your risk appetite? What is your support system in the personal life and their expectations you want to meet? Do you like to deal with ambiguity, or you are binary in approach? Are you someone who loves to have a social life, or you enjoy being on your own irrespective of the location you are in? Most importantly, what is your purpose in life and what you want to achieve through a career?

Understand What You Like

Do you like to be driven or you are a driver? Do you like working in a chaos or you like to work in a place where rules, guidelines, and systems are clear. Are you entrepreneurial in nature? How much do you yearn for recognition, or are you self-driven? Do you like to work independently or as a part of large group? Do you like to work in a secure environment only or you are fine to work in an insecure workplace? How much change is good for you and your ability to adapt to it?

Invest on a Career Coach or Mentor

Share your thoughts on who you are and what you like with a career coach or a mentor. Spend time with them, they will be able to provide you guidance beyond your ability for two reasons as they might have seen the world more than you and they will be able to help you reflect much deeper and better than you can. This is more successful if you are able to unmask yourself in front of the coach or mentor. Intermittent coaching or counselling session from a professional will help you make better choices as there are lot of things that happen in life during our journey which are unprecedented, and we are lost in terms of planning at these times the coach enables you to reduce your anxiety level and provide you a balanced perspective.

SEVEN

Leadership and Legacy

If we are asked about leaders who influenced our lives and inspired us, leaders who we want to emulate, what are the common characteristics of such leaders and why do we remember them and not others who may have been more successful, more tactful or more powerful? What is it about them that they stand out? On a quick reflection all of us would realise that these leaders had huge followers and the emotional appeal they evoke still in each of the followers while they may have moved on to a different context or phase in life.

We often tend to use the word leader casually in corporate world and use it for managers with large number of reporting. A senior manager is often called a leader, and this has been complicated even more by the designation deluge which is even more misleading.

For starters, a leader is one who has followers. If there is no one who gets inspired by your deeds, by your vision, by your direction, then you are not a leader. Authority and power vested to an individual by an organisation to drive the organisational outcomes is merely mechanisms to support administrative and functional prowess of an individual. It's a common sight in organisations that senior managers bask in the glory of these powers and in many cases think of themselves as leaders as they are taking decisions on growth development and performance of team members.

If we reflect a bit deeper, we will realise that the managers in our lives who became leaders for us are the ones who have left an indelible mark in our lives and we continue to follow them, their principles, values, style or even certain traits. In some cases, we emulate, and in certain other cases, imitate.

The characteristics of the leader who has created this legacy in the lives and organisations are often the same. An authentic self, a guiding light, an unbiased outlook, and most importantly, an ability to create more leaders. While each of the leaders may have their fair share of success and failure, but in success or failure, they have maintained these characteristics and that's what makes us remember them fondly and follow them and be a part of their legacy.

EIGHT

Leading with Trust

As we grow from an individual contributor to a manager to a manager's manager and then to leaders of organisations in our respective domains of expertise, the expectations of the organisation, the people who work with us, the shareholders, the customers, essentially all stakeholders grow leaps and bounds. Every stakeholder looks up to a leader to deliver the margins, deliver the returns, deliver the bonus for them higher year on year amidst market uncertainties, volatile economic environment, rising global competition, increasing cost pressures. One leader is entrusted with the task of beating competition by margin unheard of, one leader is entrusted with the task of reducing costs never seen before, one leader is entrusted to reduce the headcount by half as a part of restructuring. All these seem to be daunting tasks and insurmountable too in the beginning. However, as leaders if the stakeholders' expectation is that the leaders deliver to these seemingly unachievable targets, then the leaders have no choice but to roll up their sleeve and start strategizing as that's probably the only way to make the organisation sustainable as finalised by the stakeholders.

To strategize, plan, and execute these seemingly insurmountable goals the leader looks up to his team to drive the extra mile, to go the extra distance, to push themselves harder in execution of the plans strategized. The leader consistently strategizes with the team, reviews along with the team leaders, coaches the team leaders and guides the team towards the goals planned. However, it requires the belief of each team member in the purpose, in the goal, and in the leader—to go the extra mile for the leader and for the organisation—and achieve the unachievable, as they say in corporate lingo, and to dream big and deliver bigger. If we look into this phenomenon through a lens, we will realise that the art of being able to deliver extraordinary results through ordinary teams is what makes leaders great, and this entire phenomenon is possible because the teams they lead trust their leader. The team trust their leaders' beliefs, the leader's vision, and the leader's execution strategy and most importantly they trust the fact that if they deliver the extra mile for the leader then they will accomplish their professional and personal goals in the long run.

How do we develop this level of trust in the teams we lead, how can this be measured and do we get this level of trust from our teams from the day we take up a leadership position? And the most important fact, can leaders be successful if they are not able to lead their teams with trust. Well, the answer to all this lies in the simple phrase '*leadership is not about what we say; it's all about what we do*'. A leader is able to lead with trust through the actions he demonstrates to the team over a period of time. Once they see the consistency in the actions then they start trusting the leader and are willing to walk the extra mile for the leader and on lot of occasions without looking at the outcomes of the extra hours of work or the sacrifices they need to make in their personal lives to achieve the outcomes. Let's reflect on the aspects and actions that enable a leader to lead with trust.

Competence

The demonstrated behaviours of the leader both in functional and behavioural aspect should reflect the high level of knowledge, skills, experience, and exposure the leader brings to the team. The level of trust of the team increases when the leader through his/her competence is able to provide direction which no one thought of which eventually enables the team to win or troubleshoot a complex situation from which no one was able to get out and thus eventually makes the team cut their losses. A lot of time the role of the leader in enabling performance is to provide the extra fillip in terms of motivation or being the statesman who is able to troubleshoot complex situations or providing direction which towards a path which is unchartered but eventually brings laurels for the team. All these are possible only if there is a high level of competence possessed by the leader. Highly competent leaders evoke a lot of respect and trust amongst their teams.

Performance

A track record of being a solid performer in the past is a must to start off with for the leader, however the real trust develops in the team once they see that the leader is performance outcome oriented and drives them towards the performance objectives and thus enables the team to come out winner. The moment team is able to taste success of the outcomes, although on the way they might have faced hardships, the trust level on the directions provided by the leader increases. A solid performance outcome is always an outcome of great planning and flawless execution, the leader needs to oversee both these aspects strategically and tactically to enable the team to come out successful.

Integrity

Integrity is not only about the financial honesty; integrity for a leader is to be committed to the cause at all times and being accountable for the success and failure of the team. A lot of leaders fail in the fact they take the credits for all the success of the team but single out individuals in case of failures. This is one of the biggest deal-breakers to earn the trust of the teams. Integrity is also a lot about the level of fairness demonstrated in handling various business and people situations, and problems and most importantly being authentic in actions. Being political or creating a divide and rule environment in the team eventually leads to mistrust amongst team members and with the leader and thus creates a challenge to drive the team towards the goal.

Empathy

The leader should know the challenging circumstances under which the team works at time, the leader should know the hardships they face to deliver the outcomes, and the leader should be able to understand some of the intrinsic and extrinsic challenges which are deterrent to the outcomes and beyond control of team members. The leader should always have an ear to the ground level at which the last person in the hierarchy is pushing the organisation agenda. As they say it's important to understand the opportunities and challenges both of the man in the arena who is pushing the organisation agenda. The leader being aware of all these elements of on ground situation and of team members creates a sense amongst team members that the leader is aware of their situation and is enabling them, pushing them on the agenda with clear understanding of ground realities. It's thus very important to build empathy for the team and what they do by the leader to build trust. A leader who has high level of empathy will eventually also be seen by the team as caring and understanding despite being highly task oriented.

Leading with Trust is one of the key foundations of being a successful leader, teams rally behind the leaders they trust and go for many extra miles for such a leader. If you are a leader and you are hearing or seeing *'I don't trust you'* from your people, take steps now to remedy the situation, reflect on the points mentioned above, a lot of your success as a leader depends on it. Leadership is a lot about leading with Trust.

NINE

Meetings: A Contemporary Challenge at Workplace

The tag line would evince all kinds of reactions and emotions depending on each of our context situation as employees of the corporate world wherever we are in globally. Each one of us are navigating the most effective way to work amidst meeting in our corporate jobs even now.

On one such reflection moment, was wondering with all my senses on the fact that what was our life in the pre-COVID era, why did we not have so many meetings in our calendar and still performance and outcomes were driven with equal and in some cases more aplomb than now. The reflective journey led to various discoveries of the way we are working today as a group than we were. Various thoughts were crossing the mind, are the managers in post-COVID era being more control freaks or are they continuing with the control due to the unnerving impact to business of COVID and holding on to the same control mechanisms or is it that there are more disruptions than few years back and there is a need to be in more constant touch with the group than before to navigate or is it that we have got digital tools like MS Teams and Zoom which are free of cost and at times we are overusing it to connect, I am sure each of us have our own thoughts around this and dealing with the overdose of meetings in our lives. While we deal in our own way, sharing some of the key tenets, which if evaluated, probably will equip managers better with the ability to solve problems at hand:

- Meetings and reviews are collaborative tools. They enable to solve the problem, there is an action that needs to be done to solve the problem. Are we providing our teams enough time to be on the ground and deal with the problem towards solution or are we discussing more towards solutioning?
- We are well past the business continuity challenge stage, and hence can we evolve towards less control era like earlier as disruptions may be higher than before but it's not disrupting so frequently like the business continuity challenge era. Are we empowering the troops to fight the battle or are we still fighting it out like in the lockdown situation?
- In a disruptive situation or emergency all hands are required on board, everyone is required to be together and pitch in, in a continuity stage can we make our meetings smaller with the core team only and only the direct report layer unless it's a communication or engagement theme.
- Digital tools have disrupted the role of managers, specially the aggregator roles. Can we evaluate the value generation of these aggregators' roles? And if not, club the roles or remove them lest they

overburden the teams without much productive outcomes.

Like in every change there is an evolution, the business world will emerge differently as we deal with a problem, however it's important that we veer towards the solution faster as business world as there are implications on productivity, effectiveness, efficiency, and most importantly on mental and physical health of the madness of meetings.

TEN

The Role of a Leader

We are all aware of the fact that leadership is one of the key ingredients of a successful organisation. Among other things, leadership contributes in creating the culture, the vision, the business trajectory, and the talent landscapof an organisation.

Leaders assume various roles in various functions across organisations with varying degree of empowerment, centralisation, and scope based on the type of business, type of organisation, role they are playing. Some roles are more empowering than others, some roles are more powerful than the other, and some roles are more impactful than the others. Leaders grow in an organisation and across organisations by experiencing variety of such roles during their career.

There are certain commonalities around these roles. Any leadership role comes with 1) the responsibility of a manager's manager, 2) a higher sphere of influence than of authority, 3) willingness to manage teams that are distributed geographically, and 4) the ability to guide managers and inspire them.

With the above-stated context, let's understand the role of a leader. The role of a leader in any organisation can be divided into four broad dimensions discussed here.

To Provide Direction to the Function or Business

Leaders shape the direction of the organisation and teams they lead. Clarity of vision, pyramid of purpose, and strategic direction are things a leader needs to understand first and then accordingly break down the actionable for their teams accordingly. Teams look up to leaders for Direction and once the leader sets the direction with clear actionables, the managers in the team navigate the teams towards the goal.

To Coach the Managers in the Team

Managers look forward to leaders to enable them to be successful. It's important for leaders to continually coach and guide managers on various aspects of managing work and managing teams towards successful execution of goals. Managers don't need guidance to execute day to day work or deliverables, they are adept at it. Managers need constant coaching from the leader to maximise their own and team's potential towards successful outcomes. Focused approach towards coaching by leaders also enable them to grow more leaders in the organisation in future.

To Troubleshoot Problems

Managers in the team look up to a leader the most when they are stuck with a problem. Hence it's very important for a leader to play the role of a troubleshooter. Someone who can help to fix problems which are beyond the sphere of influence or beyond the understanding of the team. The role of a leader is key in troubleshooting. The leader helps to troubleshoot the issue taking the help of larger organisation. It's very important for the leader to be functionally dexterous, high on interpersonal effectiveness, and foresighted to be an able troubleshooter for the team.

To Engage with the Team

It's very important for leaders to engage with the larger teams and understand the pulse of the organisation and people they are leading. Communication forums, round tables, one-on-one sessions, reward and recognition forums, and open-door policy are some of the aspects a leader adapts to engage with his team. The perspectives that the leader gets through the various mechanisms of engagement, enable the leader to take actions in terms of people and organisation dimension and course correct at times if required or reinforce further if things are in the right direction.

ELEVEN

When Good Is Not Good Enough

In our professional lives we often come across various professionals who are in various phases of their career and who have a deep feeling of not living up to their own career aspiration due to the circumstances or the organisational support or their own personal priorities being different at some point. Being an HR professional, I have often heard from these set of professionals about how, once a star of the organisation but eventually fading away, their organisations do not value their contributions today as much as it used to earlier. There is a common theme that I have observed in this set of professionals. Each of them felt stuck in their careers due to a lack of growth opportunity inside as well as outside the organisation. Each of them complained that they had always done their best but their organisations would often calibrate them differently for the same level of performance.

On studying career journeys of such professionals closely and reflecting on how they could have done differently. The themes discussed next come to my mind which as a professional I am cognisant about for my own career as a professional and would like to share with all who are in such a phase or who want to ensure that they don't get into such a phase ever in their career.

Rolling Stone Gathers No Moss

Keep changing your role every 2-3 years be it horizontally, vertically within the function or outside the function basis the career aspiration. Moving jobs and doing different roles within the same organisation preferably add to the muscles of a professional in terms of rounded understanding and ability to evaluate a challenge or task from all dimensions which eventually leads to better decision-making and better ability to perform in a given role.

Embrace Growth Mindset

Always ready to take new challenges, learning from failure, taking bigger assignments with considerable responsibility and can-do attitude are traits of growth mindset. It's important that we build a growth mindset at all times of our career journey.

Your Career Your Responsibility

Often, employees in organisations feel that the organisation should take care of their career. Organisations do provide frameworks and growth paths for the talent; however, the reality is that corporate structures are pyramids, and all can't be accommodated as they move up. Hence, it's important that we realise that our career is our responsibility, and we work towards making the most of the organisational career development framework to ensure we either grow in the pyramid within the organisation or outside in another organisation.

Develop Competencies for the Market

A career is a long journey; the functional and behavioural competencies that enable success in an organisation at a given point of time is different from the one a few decades later. It's not because the organisation wanted to change but because the organisation was forced to change to cater to the changing dynamics of the market and varied taste of customers. Hence, it's important that we professionals consistently develop our competencies by learning and doing both to stay ahead of the curve at all times. Amounts incurred on self-development are not costs they are investments for a long successful career.

TWELVE

An Effective Leader amidst Crisis

Amidst the unprecedented situations created by the pandemic due to COVID-19, we are all responding to the crisis and dealing with the crisis in our own way. Be it in our personal life or professional life the challenges for each are a lot different and a lot similar. The similarity lies in our ecosystem and economic challenges and the difference lies in the way our families, homes, and support systems are structured.

On the professional front, the thought crossing the mind of each one of us all the time is, are we doing enough, are we managing the situation effectively at work, is there something more we can do to be more effective to the organisation and also at times the thought revolves around the fact that is it worth doing anything at all because we do not know how things will pan out in the future, because in the new normal it may not be relevant. We are also constantly worried on the outcomes of the crisis on our professional and personal aspiration. It is in these situations the role of an effective leader becomes extremely important for organisations.

An effective leader can create a huge positive impact for the organisation. The effective leader knows how to soothe the nerves in crisis, is able to provide the direction to the team, is able to keep stakeholders engaged to the cause, is able to understand the direction in which the organisation needs to shift its action and ensure that the organisational priorities are managed with utmost importance with significant level of employee engagement in the team. The impact of a leader amidst crisis can be so profound that there have been many examples in the past wherein organisations have emerged stronger out of a crisis than it was when it went into the crisis.

Let us reflect on the behaviours that enable leaders to demonstrate and create such lasting impacts during crisis:

Agile

Effective leaders are much more agile amidst crisis, they understand that unprecedented situations don't have standard recipes to manage the outcomes hence it is important to change the directions as may be required and realign the team every time, if it is required to steer the ship out of crisis. They are able to tap the opportunities that may arise due to crisis and align the team towards new outcomes in quick time as well.

Resilient

The ability to stand tall amidst crisis and not give up is always characterised by high resilience. Continuously thinking of ways and means to bounce back even when chips are down is very important. It is important to have the ability and confidence to take a step at a time every day and trudge along the path without losing faith.

Empathetic

It's important that the leader understands the difficult situations the team is going through, everyone has their own challenges in personal life, how does the leader empathise and also energise the team in such situations is a fine balance only a few have. The leader should demonstrate empathy in dealing with all the stakeholders, the customers, financers, suppliers, etc.

Vulnerable

Effective leaders communicate with a lot of humility and vulnerability, this enables the team to understand that everyone is going through the crisis together and the complimentary skills of the team is required to take the team out of the crisis, the leader when vulnerable also creates a feeling of being authentic to the team.

THIRTEEN

An Effective Way to Deal with Adversity

We are often faced with adversities that are unprecedented and completely unheard of, which can create adverse impacts on our lives. The coronavirus outbreak is definitely an adversity, which has and will have a devastating impact in terms of social and economic contexts. We all are faced with a situation, which we never thought we would. All of us are adapting to various ways of fighting the deadly virus in our daily lives wherever we are and in whichever social and economic strata we belong.

Any kind of adversity shatter each of one our aspirations, plans and at times even dreams for the time being. It creates a sense of panic in the mind and a feeling of helplessness. This often leads to a sense of anxiety and fear, and we often tend to become regressive and negative in our mindset of navigating the future and achieving the goals we have set for ourselves. We tend to lose our enthusiasm towards the goal or the purpose with which we were addressing problems or situations. The current set of adversities we are in and will undergo are no different.

The most effective way to deal with Adversity in any form in life is to build Resilience. The term resilience is all about overcoming adversity, it is about making great comebacks, it is about standing tall amidst tough situations and it's about being tough. It's one of the most important traits of a Leader in the present volatile global business and political environment. Lot of us are resilient because of our life experiences and lot of us are building resilience basis our life experiences. It's clearly a survival tactic we need to master in order to survive the ordeal of the VUCA world as a leader. Sharing a few of my perspectives on how to build resilience from my personal experiences amidst adversity will for sure keep you in good stead in the current situation and many more such situations in the days ahead.

Reflect on What Needs to Be Fixed
Reflect on the things you have set out to accomplish which got derailed and what are the things you need to do get them back on track. Make note of the aspects that need to be focussed upon in the immediate and near term.

Build a Positive Outlook
Create a can-do attitude and a thought process of there is always light at the end of the tunnel. As said, attract the positives, if you want something the universe conspires to make it happen. Keep the faith.

Get Over the Why-Me Syndrome
In case of adversities, we often feel why it has happened to me while there are so many in the world for whom it has not happened, it's a very negative and distressing thought and the biggest drawback to building resilience.

Instead reflect about people who are far less privileged than you and how they manage to keep their chin up. Life is all about enjoying the experiences it provides till it lasts, create memories with whatever you have and be thankful to the almighty.

Take One Day at a Time

In face of adversity, it's not good to prepare long term, you may not know how it will unfold further, how deep is the cut may still be unknown. Hence, it's important to make plans for near term, a week or few weeks in advance. It's like playing a test match cricket, make most of every session of play and build the outcome towards making an impact eventually. If you plan longer, then you may be disappointed soon and you may get into a negative thought process again, it is important to keep the spirits alive and hence a short term here and now executable plan to overcome the adversity is important.

Take Care of Yourself

It's important to take care of oneself, one's own health, fitness levels, and mental health. Pay attention to your own needs and feelings. Engage in activities that you enjoy and find relaxing. Exercise regularly. Taking care of yourself helps to keep your mind and body primed to deal with situations that require resilience.

FOURTEEN

Appreciative Enquiry Enables Collaborative Change

When was the last time you have seen a business leader with a know-it-all attitude, the answer to it is probably we encounter them all the time? As leaders gain experience and success this is bound to happen as they become more confident of themselves and tend to feel in control of the situation. With the rapid disruption that each of us faces today and the unprecedented changes we are witnessing around us, we may want to believe we are in control, however, it's not feasible or possible to control due to the sheer disruptive forces that are in action in each and every aspect of businesses across industries. The name of the game to thrive in the current context is collaboration and partnerships.

To enable leaders to build collaboration and partnerships to solve disruptive strategic challenges, an effective tool is appreciative enquiry. It is a process in which you continuously try to appreciate the various facets of the problem and seek answers and learn from subject matter experts. It's the process of finding the strengths in a practice process or innovative idea and thereby strengthening the understanding of the group and contributing to the overall process. Appreciative enquiry enables to move towards a shared vision by engaging others in strategic innovation. Appreciative enquiry is used for driving collaborative change and building agile organisations. It communicates strategic challenges effectively by seeking inputs from a group on the various dimensions of the problem.

The collaborative problem-solving process involves all stakeholders into the problem and the process of solutioning. It creates commitment and enables to drive change much more effectively. Stakeholders, due to the involvement and commitment generated in the process of appreciative enquiry, are also much more willing to stretch beyond the means and absorb the pains for the greater good of the organisation which they have appreciated in the process. It thus also enables a much greater collaboration amongst team members and within the various parts of the organisation as they are all in it together.

To make appreciative-enquiry-based transformations successful the leader needs to also adapt towards a collaborative decision-making process, often it may seem that a collaborative decision-making process on important aspects is slowing down the entire process of outcomes, however contrary to the popular belief the commitment to the change that the process drives is much more faster than actual change through a sudden decision-making process or of a decision taken by a leadership team. Another important characteristic that the leader needs to hone to make the transformation successful, if the mode is AI, is humility and vulnerability; it will enable the leader to seek collaboration and appreciate the various dimensions of the solutioning process.

Often we see leaders very resistant to the ideas, while they hear the ideas, listen to the idea, they don't act on the idea of the group or team members, it's because they feel that their past experiences have taught them differently, however in the process they forget that the past is in no way a reflection of the future, the future problems needs futuristic solutions and not proven in the past solutions.

With collaboration being the way forward to drive success in the organisations of tomorrow, appreciative enquiry is one of the key tools that will enable organisations to shape the future and drive organisation development.

FIFTEEN

Careers Are Marathons, Enjoy the Journey

If you like running marathons, you'll realise that it really doesn't matter which part of the marathon you run fast or which part you run slow, what matters is how much time you have clocked to close the marathon, and most importantly, the satisfaction of being able to run the full distance of the marathon within the time line we have set for ourselves. The latter is much more important than the former.

For the last 3 years, I have been running long distances and often almost daily. One thing that I have realised, that every day is different, every run has its own characteristics, be it for the weather, be it for the physical condition of mine, be it my mental makeup on the day, be it for the surroundings in which I am running, etc. etc. Someday I run first few kilometres with high speed, in some I run the last few with high speed and for every run the middle is the most difficult part of the run always. There are various factors which determine and shape the character of the long run each day and each day is different. There are similar days but never the same day.

While you are running, it enables you to concentrate and think about various aspects in a focused manner, many runners equate it with the state of meditation, on one such thought-provoking moment being an HR profession I started comparing the marathons with careers. While making the comparison, the more I introspect, the more the similarities emerged. I am sharing some of the thoughts that crossed my mind and hope you find it relevant for yourself.

- Like each marathon, every individual's career is different. Each one of us have our own journey because of our own aspirations, realities, contexts, and destinies. Careers can be similar but not the same as marathons. Every journey is unique.
- Like marathons, the most important aspect of career is how much you enjoyed the journey and the satisfaction of completing the journey successfully as planned in the beginning. After you run few miles in career you realise that it's important to pace it right and enjoy if you got to finish the marathon, else there is a chance of burning out and not able to complete the marathon and reach the career destination.
- Like marathons, in careers as well, it doesn't matter if you have done the first half faster or the second half faster, what matters is eventually how much time you clocked at an overall level and what's the distance you traversed. Plan the glide path of the career like the marathon with the full distance in mind and do not get paranoid about speed or destinations in the short runs, we need to look at how we are reaching the eventual milestone of the career.

- Like marathons, in careers as well, it's the middle that is the most difficult period, wherein either you are tired if you have run the first half fast or you have realised you are slow and you need to run the second half faster and in both cases in the middle you want to take a breather and often feel like getting disenchanted. Like in marathons, in careers as well, it's in the middle you need to strengthen your mind to drive much more strongly towards the desired outcome and avoid the distractions towards the successful completion of the journey. Many get derailed during the middle both in marathons and careers and hence it's important to know your derailer and plan the strategy to overcome it.
- Like in marathons, in careers as well, success comes to those who are determined, are high on resilience, and has a disciplined approach. Seldom in marathons or careers will a person with low resilience, low determination, and low discipline will ever be successful. Resilience, discipline, and determination always take you miles both in marathon and careers.
- Like in marathons, in careers as well, it doesn't matter who ran past you or who ran behind you, it's your marathon, it's your career, enjoy the journey, pace it right as you have decided to and not as it's decided by others. Competitive mindset is important, and it enables better speed both in marathons and careers; however, we have to know our game well and pace it right for ourselves to make it to the eventual destination with the timing we wanted when we started our journey.

SIXTEEN

Fostering Innovation: Creating a Culture of Embracing Failure

A lot has been told in the last 36 hours post the last mile failure of the Chandrayan project of ISRO on how to embrace failure, how important it is to take up failure in the positive spirit and how leaders should motivate at times of failure like our honourable Prime Minister has done. And the fact that it's the true essence for fostering a culture of innovation. LinkedIn, Twitter, and many social media platforms are abuzz with tons of messages congratulating ISRO and letting them know that the nation is Proud of their achievements even with the last-mile failure. It was such a great day for humanity and leadership to be unleashed and for the power of science to be celebrated.

Amidst all this, the reflection naturally came in the form of a thought, that how we create a culture of embracing failure in an organisation because only when we create such a culture then only the employees and leaders of the organisation will be embarking on task as audacious and futuristic as ISRO had set out to do or has almost done. In the world of business today wherein digital disruption of business models is a way of life, bringing in innovation and disruptive technologies to mainstream is the only way to survive for organisations. Thus, it's important even more for organisations to foster a culture of innovation and risk taking and thus a culture of embracing failures.

It's definitely easier said than done in organisations, in the business world the shareholders are tracking financial performance quarter on quarter, stock markets react to failures on daily basis, lenders are validating each and every ROI model before investing and most importantly during the year-end appraisal the manager is more interested to evaluate the results and not efforts. With so much working against a small blip in performance outcomes, failure of a big project or in a big project is often perceived to be either a slowdown in career or an indication to move on to another organisation. Isn't this a recipe for disastrous outcomes for the organisations in the long run? If it is then how do we create cultures of embracing failure amidst the business realities as stated above and the constant reminder that cash is king.

A few things an organisation can consider doing to foster a culture that embraces failure and thereby creates a culture of innovation and risk taking.

- Create a safety net for all those who are part of a project or task that are high risk oriented. Ensure the team is told in the very beginning that they would be evaluated on how committed they are on the tasks assigned and not so much on the outcomes as the project or task is a high risk and high gain one. The more we build safety nets for such projects, we would see employees and leaders stretching themselves more and we would see a more risk-taking approach.

- Encourage diversity of perspectives. Often, leaders, in an autocratic manner, shun the views and ideas of their subordinates with a clear message: 'I know how to get this done here.' The leaders should at all times encourage diverse point of views and ideas within the team and let the team experiment and evaluate the outcomes in a calculated manner. It's not advised to encourage the team in taking blind risks but a calculated risk on a different way of pursuing an outcome or trying out new things. Doing this go a long way in encouraging innovation. In case of failure in doing things the new way, the leader should be open to encourage the team and focus on learnings that the process brought about and thereby derive from the learnings.
- A mechanism of Recognising employees or teams who have made a difference by taking risks or innovating for the organisation although it may not have met with desired outcomes.
- A continuous leadership communication in a structured way in all discussions with employees and subordinates that it's fine to fail if there is enough effort and within the framework of calculated risk.

As the saying goes, culture is all about what leaders do, hence it's important for organisational leadership to walk the talk and embrace failures of teams who have been audacious and risk takers in the true spirit of innovation and in the pursuit of being a game changer and thereby foster a culture of innovation in the organisation. There is no mathematical or simulation model to evaluate it, it needs leadership prudence to make it happen.

SEVENTEEN

Creating a More Effective Learning: Interventions in Digital Mode

It's been 6 months now that the dreaded pandemic struck us in India, with the lockdowns and consequent reopening of the economy, we have gone into a frenzy of operating in digital mode in almost everything including imparting training and capability-building initiatives. Every programme that was being done physically is being reworked in a digital mode. It is the right way to do now because it is a survival tactic more than anything else. We are unaware of how long this would go on and hence till the time the situation remains the way it is today we need to continue to strive to build the capability initiatives in a digital mode and refine the effectiveness parameters. Based on my experience of attending programmes in digital mode and designing programmes in a digital mode, summing up some of the key aspects to reflect upon while working on designing a learning programmes in the digital mode.

Distractions are High in Digital Mode
Ensure that programmes are conducted for smaller duration as it is not always possible to focus digitally for

longer duration. It is important that the participant takes it seriously and is involved like it is in the classroom. Ensure the video mode is on so that the participants provide required attention all the time and create required set up at workplace or home to enable learning.

Engagement Is the Key

Ensure smaller groups of participants for higher level of engagement; it is very difficult to engage in a focussed manner with more than 12 participants in a digital mode. Create the curriculum with enough engagement initiatives during the programme. Higher engagement will ensure more effective transfer of learning. Various forms of engagement like group work, quiz, role play, extempore, etc., can be worked out to ensure engagement.

Infrastructure Set-up Check Is Important

It is very important to do a dummy run along with participants and spell out the infra requirements before the programme starts. Else there are cases when a few participants are not able to follow the pace of the group and a lot of back and forth needs to be done during the programme. Support with additional infra if required to participants; build the additions in programme cost.

Pre-work Review Is a Value Add

Lot of times we assume participants have done the necessary pre-work, since the transfer of learning is a bit of an issue in digital mode. It would be good if there is pre-work review and discussion session created specifically for learnings from pre-work before we start the programme.

Avoid Topics That Require Experiential Learning
Postpone programmes as much possible which require experiential learning, while there can always be a logic of the programme can be done digitally, certain programmes which require intense participation of the body and mind to experience certain concepts, traits, or feelings, it's best to wait a while till we can conduct classroom more effectively.

EIGHTEEN

Effective Performance Management System

Performance management system or PMS is said to be one of the most important levers that differentiates a great organisation from a good organisation. It is a function of various things of an organisation, its intent, its objectives, the values, the culture. The ethos, the reward philosophy, and most importantly its people. All the components mentioned are wide subjects in their own sense and have a varied and diverse implications for each organisation. To assimilate all this into one system without diluting the essence or importance of any one of them is a daunting task.

The how part of superior performance outcomes that is the demonstrated behavioural indicators called competencies for one industry is very different from another industry. The winning competencies in an automobile company are not only very different from a power company but also from another automobile company as well of different vintage and different ownership pattern. Thus, PMS is one of the most contextual processes of and for an organisation. The principles and practices of an excellent PMS in a great organisation may not be the ingredient for success for another organisation, hence mere copying of practices or processes in this arena shall lead to utter failure and disoriented organisational approaches.

This eventually leads us to the discussion on variables based on which a great PMS is designed. How can we ensure that PMS is effective? What are the factors that would vary based on organisations and industries that we need to keep in mind? How do we keep the organisation context in mind? How would values be reflected through the performance management system? How to drive accountability till the last mile in the organisation. How do we ensure that we do not label employees for life on the basis of one performance cycle? The mere mention of so many distinct variables makes us feel that it's indeed a great puzzle worth solving for an organisation and for all of us HR professionals.

The biggest conundrum while designing an effective PMS is to balance subjectivity and objectivity. While purists may say that it should be fully objective and then it would evolve into a fair and just process, the fact remains that this is a people process; it involves humans and not machines, and also organisations run performance management system to enhance performance, thus development should also be a key input of it; hence the exact calibration of all humans in the same yardstick is in reality an impossible task. This leads us to think that we should then try to be as accurate as possible in this sojourn and hence devise a PMS which has a good blend of accountability orientation and development driven.

An accountability-driven PMS is clearly one that takes the overall objective of the organisation into consideration and is able to further break it down into various functional and sub-business objectives. Once these objectives are finalised, it's important to pen down key performance indicators (KPI) to meet the objectives. A SMART approach to writing the KPI enables to understand the lead indicators of performances during the various reviews done month on month. It is important to ensure that for all functions and sub-functions these are aligned to the overall objectives. Better the alignment of the KPI even better is the ability to measure the outcomes and thus accountability of the PMS.

A development-driven PMS is clearly one which enables development discussions between a manager and subordinate based on the behaviours demonstrated vis-à-vis the winning competencies of the organisation on a continuous basis focusing on what the subordinate needs to continue or consider going forward. The outcomes of these development discussions should be followed through by a great set of talent development initiatives built around the 3E concept: experience, exposure, and education.

For driving accountability and continuous development in an employee or a set of employees requires an effective manager with the leadership skills to inspire, motivate, engage, and drive. Thus, eventually driving a great performance management system is all about having effective managers who are great coaches as well.

Does that mean that performance management after so much of objective crunching, goal alignments, development discussions, competency mappings is all about the quality of leaders in the organisation driving it? Does that mean a PMS can be effective only if the organisation has great leaders? Is there no merit in a great system design or is it the case that an organisation can only succeed if it has great leaders? Well, the answer is yes and no? Yes, because it's only when you have managers who have leadership skills you can drive a great performance management system and no because the effective manager with great leadership ability may not be able to steer the outcomes or coach in the best manner if not given a well-designed PMS with inherent coaching to him/her on how to drive it effectively.

Thus, to sum it up, for an effective performance management system in an organisation, it requires a fine blend of accountability and development-led design, which is then to be executed by an effective set of managers who are also great coaches.

NINETEEN

Crystal Gazing: Emerging Trends in HR

As practitioners in a function, we are so caught up in the here and now, the monthly, the yearly, the scorecard, the next pay rise, the incentive, etc., we often tend to overlook at the trends emerging to ride the future waves of growth as professionals and organisation. The changeover is less painful always if it is gradual and intrinsic; the changeover is enjoyable if it is done as a part of growing up and not as a part of survival tactic. To enable for a gradual and proactive changeover, it's important that we are aware of the emerging trends, the next wave or the next big thing.

Managed time to reflect on the emerging trends in human resource basis my experience and understanding, sharing some of my thoughts, which I will be working on in order to avoid being fossilised as a professional 10–15 years from now.

From a social context point of view with more and more Gen Z coming to workplace, the first set of truly digital natives at workplace, the ones who are used to internet, social networks, digital communities, the ones who don't need to read an encyclopaedia to know the truth and its different versions, the ones who are born in an age of growth and consumerism, the one who believes in less saving and one life to live, how do the workplace need to change for them in order to attract them, get the best out of each them. With such attributes of the employee, it is imperative the practices of human resources will tend to change, the definition of great place to work will change and so will be the competencies of a great people manager and HR leader.

From a business context, with the advent of technology, there have been major developments towards creating a digital outlook in organisations and the role of AI in driving outcomes, be it in operations or consumer-facing business. Today, there is a consensus that 'data is the new oil.' What it drives businesses towards is aggregation and analytics. If businesses are to be driven by aggregation and analytics, the way people will be managed will also be influenced by these changes.

Keeping the social and business context in mind, these are few of the trends that have emerged from my reflection, which I feel will emerge in the area of human resource function in the days ahead:

- A flat and less hierarchical organisation with high level of transparency and meritocracy will be the bare minimum. What will be valued is flexibility, encouragement of diversity of thoughts and backgrounds both, ethical work practices and environment friendly. Values and culture have to be redefined gradually basis the need of the hour and organisations driven accordingly.

- Talent will not be forever; talent will work for roles or assignments until the challenge is of interest to them both professionally and personally, and hence will lay the foundation for the gig-talent economy. Career paths and succession maps may become obsolete.
- AI will replace surveys and FGD and machine-learning-based barometers to predict the behaviour trends and solutions will also be customised basis the trends. Mass approach may not be of use as digital will enable customised output which today is not feasible. One-time engagement surveys, or mood indicators, will not be in need and may need to be reborn in a different way.
- Analytics based on analytics of employee behaviour data points will be one of the key functions in HR that will generate the decision points on HR initiatives for the organisation. HR decisions will be more fact based than emotion based today.
- Talent attraction will be community based. Talent acquisition teams will work on being a part or creating broad talent communities and continuously engaging with them for various assignments that will emerge for the next gig role.
- Talent development will be much more personal in nature and microlearning will emerge as a more acceptable form of learning than the ILT or LMS, which are in vogue today.

TWENTY

Enable and Enforce: A Critical Balance for an Effective HR Leader

The role of an HR leader for an organisation is constantly evolving. From being a business enabler, it is slowly evolving towards being a business partner. Higher frequency of disruptions in business environment is creating change management as an important element for businesses to survive and thrive. A major aspect of change management involves changing mindsets of people who work in the business and at times long in the same roles doing the same things. Due to this, the business leaders are looking up to the HR function to partner with them in driving the business agenda which a decade ago was not the scenario.

As the role of HR evolves from being a business partner to a change agent of an organisation, a key dilemma for all HR professionals is how to strike a balance between being an enabler who supports business effectively and an enforcer who is able to drive change by changing cultural tenets in the organisation. Playing the dual role of being an enabler and enforcer can be very challenging as there may be times when the business leader who has looked at the HR leader as an enabler is being enforced upon due to him or her being resistant to the change that he or she has been vocal about making. Recently, an HR leader provided a very interesting anecdote of the dilemma he faced. He said that his business leaders want to change everything but do nothing. It is a very common phenomenon in organisations with legacy wherein leaders understand the need to change and work towards the same; however, when it comes to making tough calls, they shy away as they too are employees who at times are driven by emotions and tenured relationships.

Balancing between being an enabler and enforcer is a dilemma HR leaders will have to live for now in order to thrive in the business world of today and days ahead. Based on my experience of working in various organisations and contexts, here is a summary of few things HR professionals can keep in mind to handle the dilemma better. This is a skill which will evolve with more experience of handling difficult dilemma situations, hence all of us are improving as days progress and as we experience.

Keep the Problem Issue-based and Not Person-based

Drive home the point that you are having a challenge on the issue which is creating the dilemma. Provide the business leader perspective on the larger malaise that has potential to create trouble for the organisation if unattended and how it is creating challenge to drive the desired culture.

Ensure Both the Roles Are Being Played in a Balanced Manner

An enforcer role without being the enabler will create challenge of credibility for the HR leader. Hence providing value to business is of utmost importance as being the conscience keeper. Keep looking for avenues to enable and build credibility. Support business in times of distress.

Build Empathy and Listening Skills as Strengths

Change is difficult. It's not an easy proposition for many who have lived life for long in a certain way and in a certain culture. With the world around them turning around, a bit of empathy and listening skills may enable in making the change management a bit more human and also will provide a scope to them for explaining from their perspective.

Strong Business Knowledge Is the Key

A strong business knowledge will enable the HR leader with understanding of the business situation, levers to be driven and how to play the role of enabler and enforcer better. It also enables empathy and appreciation. It always enables to provide a seat on the table.

Be Brave

To play the role of an enforcer, a change agent, there may be times when the HR leader might be on the receiving end due to resistance to change of business leaders or certain group of managers influencing the business leader against the HR leader for vested interest as HR is playing the role of enforcer or there is simply resistance to change, etc. In such situations it's important to be brave and face the challenge with a clear communication and expectations and not get bog down under pressure; if you do get bog down, chances are you will never be able to drive the agenda of change or enforce change that are part of the larger mandate, and eventually, the blame of not enforcing the mandate will be on the HR leader. In such situations, it's important to remain brave and take the risk to enforce because if you are not brave you probably will not remain effective any more in the system. There might be collateral damage in the short term, but the risk, if long-term views are not taken, will remain high anyway.

TWENTY-ONE

If Humans Are a Resource, Do We Account for Talent?

Introduction of the Need

For ages now the function dealing with people-related aspects is being called the HR function, courses around the globe dealing with people, culture, and organisations are being termed as HR courses. Essentially, we are all attuned to the fact that humans are a resource in the world of doing business. Add to it various leaders of different stature, culture, and background of business talking about people-first strategies to deliver the business outcomes of an organisation as people are the most important resource in an organisation to deliver the outcomes. Human is indeed a resource for doing business.

While we are used to referring Human as Resource and the most important resource in an organisation, do we really act and enable our organisational processes and practices to believe in it or is it a lip service we have been used to doing and hence we are continuing. If we ask this basic question across organisations, many, specially the more evolved ones, will take us through 10 different things to prove they really walk the talk on the belief that humans are a resource for the business and the people its first strategy all the time. We will get to know of human resource development practices, talent attraction and management practices, diversity and inclusion practices, employee wellness practices and many more that each of them practices, to genuinely deal with people as the most important and a key resource for organisational growth and development.

If we go deeper into each of the talent management and development practices of large organisations, we will find there is one distinct difference in the way we deal with the human resource vis-à-vis the other resources of the organisation like money, materials, property, etc. That key difference being the accounting practices and principles being used. While many will instantly revert, that people are not commodities and let's not put numbers to human talent and our processes are indeed strong enough to separate the better from best and we have the ability to groom the leaders we need to do business in future. The questions that will remain in the minds of businessmen are as follows: do we have the CAGR of the organisation's talent index (how have we grown on it year on year); do we know how much resources we have lost or gained YoY; do we know by how many times have we been able to grow the talent of the organisation following our investment in people-development initiatives, and thus the ROI of investments made on people development and talent initiatives? Isn't it natural that every businessman would want to know the growth of its most important resource and its ROI?

Let us now look at how can we evolve the talent-accounting principles of an organisation and effectively make the intangibles more and more tangible for the businessman who is investing in the resource. The easier approaches to measure ROI of people practices being used for years now across industries both old and new is the improvement in productivity and efficiency in the utilisation of human resources. The key challenge in these approaches is that these measures are macro in approach and provide a point of view of the human resource effectiveness and efficiency like the financial ratios being used in accounting, however they do not provide enough perspective on all the indexes through which human resource, i.e., talent, is to be accounted and evaluated in an organisation. Like for financial resources there are various financial ratios each providing the window to a certain aspect of the financial resource and thus depicting the health of the business from that aspect, similarly for human resources as well we need to have various talent ratios which would provide a perspective and understanding of the talent aspects and thus depicting the health of the business from that aspect.

In the next chapter we will get into the details of the talent ratios of how to measure them and what perspectives they provide of the organisation.

What's an Organisation All About?

Organisation designs are done based on the very basic need to meet the customer demands and expectation on the product or services delivered. An organisation is the sum total of roles that need to be done to meet the customer demands. An organisation from the very beginning through its various stages of growth is consistently restructured to cater to the changing demands and requirements of the customer and thereby the changes in organisation design and changes in the content and number of roles. Lot of times due to changing economic conditions or market pressures and not necessarily organisation growth phase the roles are restructured in numbers and content as well to enable better outcomes. How we want the communication to happen between these roles in an organisation, how do we want the decision flow to happen between the roles in an organisation or how do we want the interactions to happen between one role to the other or to many are the other elements of an organisation's design. In essence, a lot about an organisation, be its design, culture, value or competency, hinges on two things: the role and the role holder.

The role and role holder being two most important tenets of an organisation bring us back to the discussion that if humans are resource, then a role is what the resource does; therefore, the measures of ROI of people should be around the cost of doing a role by the role holder. To arrive at the correct cost of doing a role the first step is defining the role, what is the impact that role creates, what are the kind of knowledge levels that the role needs to bring to the table, what are the organisational risks that the role will handle, what levels of innovation does this role need to bring about, these are some of the broad contours on which the role is defined, there are various methods in the industry today through leading job evaluation agencies who does help us to understand the price of the role holder which is essentially the cost of doing the role by the role holder our two most important tenets in an organisation. We are able to get what the market is paying for the job at an average on the higher side and the lower side as well.

It's for the organisations to decide how competitive in terms of attracting talent they want to be, they need to infer at market positioning for each role by combining their employee value proposition (EVP), total reward philosophy (TRP), and budgetary constraints. Through the job evaluation process the organisation will be able to measure the ideal or optimal cost of each role keeping in mind their EVP, TRP, and ability to pay.

Since an organisation is the sum total of all roles in the organisation, the costs thereby for each of these roles together summed up is essentially what the ideal human resources cost of that organisation should be bearing in their business plans for the year. It will also be the ideal cost for the human resources for the overall operational cost for the organisation.

For an organisation which has decided on market positioning at 75th percentile of the market pay for each role, the total human resource cost for that organisation need to be the total of each these roles pegged at 75th percentile. But if you go through organisational data in various organisations of different sizes, industries, and culture you will observe that in reality there are many variations from that and it does not matter if you peg the pay out at 75th percentile or 25th percentile for each role there will be variations in both types of organisations in terms of the overall cost of the all the roles vis-à-vis the sum based on market mapping at a specific percentile pay-out. In fact, in most organisations we may realise that for large number of roles for years there hasn't been any market mapping done or job evaluation done in recent past. While the dynamics of the market, hot skills, economy, job market all are fluid and continuously changing organisations at times are averse to doing a job evaluation exercise or compensation benchmarking exercise periodically. There are lot of reasons why it happens in an organisation and why something as simple as this is not done on a consistent basis. Let us reflect on the reasons for the inconsistency:

It's a Lot of Hard Work, Time Consuming, and Costly Process
Job evaluation or compensation benchmarking are time-consuming exercises. If there is a systematic approach and a good HRIS set-up, then compensation benchmarking is still far lesser time consuming than job evaluation. Hence in many progressive organisations we may see a compensation benchmarking exercise on a more periodic basis. Both these processes require a lot of hard work in terms of relooking and revisiting each role in an organisation, its description, its construct, the market competitive scenario. It's also a costly process as for sure there would be need for resources to synthesise this input, revalidate them, put it in a uniform metric, evoke discussions with various departmental heads, unit heads, and business leaders. To do all this by resources involve cost of resource and cost of time of managers and leaders involved in this process.

All of Us React to Any Change in Our Organisations
Whenever anything in an organisation is done to relook or revisit or revalidate there is trepidation that is associated with it which is a normal human behaviour. Everyone is

worried on the implication it has in it for me and my role. This in turn creates a sense of anxiety and lot of times creates a sense of disengagement and insecurity amongst employees. Due to this reason many times business leaders of an organisation resist undertaking this exercise periodically as they feel it may create an unnecessary flutter in the organisation, an unnecessary rhythm breaker to a smooth rhythm of the business and it's not worth the pain. Because of this reason we often witness such exercises being done when an organisation is going through a downturn, huge competitive pressures are there, the organisation is searching for answers within, market share loss scenario, etc.

We Have Been Managing People for Years and We Know How It Works

Lots of business leaders resist this kind of scientific approach due to the belief that they know it all, and it's more an art than science and hence such time-consuming and resource-intensive process need not be undertaken in the organisation. Apart from this sometimes the resistance from business leaders is also due to the ability of this process to put things in so much black and white perspective that it becomes a bit of a challenge to manage the grey.

Thus, it's important to understand all the above-mentioned constraints and as a leadership team arrives at a periodicity of both compensation benchmarking and job evaluation. Compensation benchmarking needs to be done more frequently than job evaluation for obvious reasons, and it's important to arrive at the periodicity for both at a leadership level to ensure consistency and also negate deliberations every time this is being done and most importantly once it is seen as a routine by employees the reaction to change will slowly disappear as it's not a change but routine and thus the negative emotions around it.

In the last part, we shall be further focusing on talent-accounting practices and talent ratios that can be looked at for effective management of human resource of an organisation. Stay tuned for more.

Financial References for an Organisation

Before we get into talent-accounting practices an organisation should be looking towards and the kind of talent ratios to ensure a strong talent management system. Let us look at what are some of the key accounting and financial parameters a businessman is interested and what all can be the corresponding one for talent, it may not be the same as its financially but having a sense of the financial perspective will provide an understanding on the aspects that the business leaders and investors continuously review and their essence to the business.

Three Golden Rules of Financial Accounting

- Debit what comes into business and credit what goes out of it.
- Debit the receiver and credit the giver.
- Debit expenses or loss to business and credit income or gains to business.

Some Aspects of Financial Management

- A P&L statement to see the overall annual profit or loss in terms of finance

- A cash flow statement to evaluate the flow of funds and an organisation's liquidity and how money moved in the system
- Debt to equity ratio that provides insights into an organisation's ability to leverage financially
- A balance sheet is a financial statement that provides a snapshot of what a company owns and owes as well as the amount invested by shareholders
- A return on capital employed is the primary measure of how efficiently a company utilises all available capital to generate additional profits

Talent Accounting and Talent Ratios

Like the financial health of an organisation, let us evaluate aspects that can provide the talent health of an organisation.

Talent P&L Statement

The talent P&L statement provides a perspective on the overall cost that an organisation should have incurred on talent versus the overall cost the organisation is incurring on talent.

Talent P&L statement = sum of total cost to the company for all positions in the organisation − sum total of the total cost to the company for all positions as per most recent job evaluation and comp benchmarking basis targeted market positioning.

The talent P&L statement will clearly provide a perspective to the stakeholders on the effective utilisation of talent in the organisation, if the organisation is growing talent effectively to develop them to take on higher responsibilities and if the organisation is continuously building leaders from within or they are buying talent often at senior leadership level. A negative talent P&L for the organisation will need to be analysed thoroughly and the reason for the same needs to be evaluated, is it due to employees overgrowing in the same role for years due to talent stagnation, its due to the inability to build leaders from within thus paying higher costs for leaders at senior level from competition or market or is it that the organisation is not able to attract talent due to ineffective EVP and thus has to shell out more cash to attract and retain both.

Talent Transition Statement
This statement provides a perspective on the talent movement into higher roles in the organisation and thus providing a perspective of eventual talent growth in the system. It clearly signifies the outcome of the talent development initiatives. This statement also provides perspective on the say do ratio of the succession plans of the organisation.

Talent transition statement = total no. of talent moved into higher level roles in a year + percentage of roles mapped under succession plans filled up internally.

Talent Balance Sheet
The talent balance sheet provides perspective on the details of the assets and liabilities for the organisation in terms of talent.

The talent balance sheet should contain the list of talent as per the defined organisational standard of talent at each level. For this it is important to define what or who is a talent for the organisation and continuously revisit this based on the changes in organisation and market dynamics. The talent balance sheet should provide details of all critical roles in the organisation and the succession maps for them. The most important aspect that the talent balance should provide is the ability of the organisation to take of the next 5-year talent requirements through its talent bench strength. It should reflect the ability of the organisation to estimate the talent requirements of its next 5-year business plan and thereby the talent availability within to fulfil its requirements.

Return on Development Initiatives Ratio
This ratio provides details on the return on the development interventions done. The ratio can be obtained by dividing the total number of mid-and senior-level positions filled up internally versus the total number of mid-and senior-level positions for which hiring was done in a particular year. This ratio provides a clear perspective on the outcome of the development interventions over the years by the organisation. Are they directed in the right direction basis the organisational need and market requirements? Are the programmes designed with an outside in perspective? Is there an effectiveness monitoring post the development interventions are rolled out?

Lastly, the talent golden rules for people and managers to be followed and encouraged across an organisation are:
- People leaders need to be talent magnets who continuously attract and retain talent for the organisation.
- Talent is for the organisation; it needs to be shared across units, departments and business for better

development of talent and more effective development of leaders in the organisation.
- Talent classification is not permanent. Talent benchmark and definition need to be consistently defined and revisited by the organisation periodically basis the market and organisational dynamics.

TWENTY-TWO

It's Time We Rename HR

The HR function in an organisation is widely perceived as the custodian of people-related process and system of the organisation. Anything to do with people is tagged with HR, be it talent management, performance management, employee relations, talent acquisition or talent development; hence, rightly so, the function has been termed as human resource management.

In the evolution process of the HR role in an organisation, today the human resource function is expected to deliver on two aspects, namely people and organisation. With the rapid pace of change due to various socio-economic factors and globalisation of the economies across the world, organisations today need to change and evolve at much faster pace than ever before. The life cycle for organisations to remain relevant in a particular industry without changing has decreased significantly, it is due to this reason unlike earlier, now the HR leadership of the organisation works along with the business leaders to manage and evolve the organisation as well towards the new paradigm of the respective industry to remain competitive.

Irrespective of the industry or the organisation or the legacy of the organisation, each organisation today is working towards how to make the organisation more effective, how to realign the organisation with the needs of the new digital world, how to create a culture for talent in the organisation across generations (diversity in nature delivers organisational needs), how to structure the organisation better to respond to customers much faster than ever before, how to drive change in cultural tenets to create a much more agile organisation? The role of a CHRO today is geared more towards driving these organisational imperatives. Today, people processes and systems are table stakes for a CHRO. They are being managed by the teams below the CHRO, and the CHRO typically would work towards aligning these people processes and systems with the organisational imperatives as stated before. It is also because of this the role of HR is becoming much more important in the organisation than ever before. Human resources leaders are not only the custodian of people processes and systems, they are also partners to business leaders in driving organisational change, enabling organisational culture and creating effective organisational structures and driving its renewal.

Not all organisations have evolved into the same dimension in terms of the role that HR teams play in their organisations. However, most of the organisations want to create HR teams that can handle both people- and organisation-related imperatives. It will not be possible for the organisation to sustain in the long run if the HR team doesn't work along with the business leader on the organisational imperatives.

Keeping the organisational imperative in mind, should we not rename the HR function as 'people and organisation management'? Critics may question this move, but it doesn't matter because:

- It's important for the stakeholders to understand the role of the HR function in the organisation and set the expectations accordingly. Today, while the business leaders understand this change in delivery of expectation, but the people manager largely is yet to understand to the extent it is required and hence the perceived value proposition of HR in the eyes of people manager is lower than with the business leader.
- The HR team in each organisation can be realigned accordingly. While CHROs or HR leaders may drive the overall agenda, be it in centres of excellence teams or business HR teams, there should be specialists who have the capability and knowledge to enable the leaders to navigate the chartered path.
- The capabilities of HR teams need to be developed accordingly. These are new skill sets, some of which are known but many new tools and techniques have evolved in the organisational management area. Focussed efforts need to be made to develop the teams.
- It's important to develop the goals of the HR function and teams accordingly. Although a lot of work happens around the organisation, the goals are still tilted towards people.

As a practitioner, it's my strong belief that we rename the HR function to people and organisation management function. Let me know your thoughts.

TWENTY-THREE

Leadership Series: Decision-Making

Often, as leaders we are with situations in which we need to take a decision for solving a complex problem the organisation is facing. The outcome of such decisions can go either way in terms of creating further trouble in the system or permanently solving a complex problem. There is a no other way out. It is in these situations that the decision-making ability and leadership values of a leader is tested.

The easier reaction to such a problem is not to stir a hornet's nest but to continue on; it's the safest choice and probably the reason the problem remained unattended, which allowed the situation to gain such gigantic and harmful proportions. The often-repeated adage in such a situation is 'will see if anything happens'.

The reason it's the most opted option is because it enables the leader not to be impacted adversely, be it in the business result or personal credibility for a cause for which he/she was not responsible. A lot of times, it's because the manager of the leader would not appreciate the dimension of the problem; addressing it then becomes risky if the outcome is not conducive; it could land the leader in trouble; hence, it's better left unattended till it hits back on the face of the organisation.

This is a situation many organisations face, and it looks up to its leaders to solve them and ensure the sustainability of the organisation.

How do we ensure that the leader concerned in the organisation takes the right decision every time which is in the best interest of the organisation and not look at the safe option? How do we groom such leaders in the organisation? Is there a training programme we can send or a role which enable this competency of a leader? The answer to it lies in the deep-rooted beliefs of the leaders in the organisation which are called values and which when collectively practised is called the culture of the organisation. Yes, it's the organisation culture only that can enable that leaders take the right decision in the best interest of the organisation every time the leader takes a decision.

While we may mistakenly consider decision-making as an individual attribute, in reality, how leaders make decisions in an organisation is deeply rooted in the culture of the organisation. An organisation culture that provides the safety net to a leader for taking the right decision even though the impact/ outcome of the decision in short term can be detrimental to the organisation will foster such decisions by its leaders. A culture in which there is high ownership for the long-term organisational goals will enable such decision-making. Thus, it's important we curate the cultural North Star of the organisation and continuously harness those cultural priorities to enable leaders do the right things and be selfless in their decision-making.

TWENTY-FOUR

Learning Is Personal and Capability Development Is Organisational

How often have we had heard or used the word training programme interchangeably for learning intervention or capability development initiative or for workshop towards organisation development? The answer would be more often or most often till a few years back. With the advent of digital tools and techniques into our learning curriculums, with the advent of YouTube-based videos for troubleshooting, with the usage of WhatsApp for sharing interesting presentations, with us attending webinars to gain knowledge on important topics, with us going through simulation techniques on our laptops or iPads, with podcasts happening globally slowly across levels and functions in organisations we have started believing in the fact that training programme is not the panacea for all development-oriented initiatives and most importantly realising that learning is location or medium agnostic and not necessarily requires to be instructor-led training programme for the best impact.

This is a change in the right direction as for many years we have not emphasised or valued the importance of learning styles or methodologies of transfer of learning into our learning curriculum as corporations, as much as we should have done. The digital age has enabled us to break various myths on how people learn and also strengthen the impetus of learning styles and methodologies of transfer of learning in our learning design frameworks. We now believe much more than ever before that all of us learn differently (e.g., some by reflecting, some by doing, some by writing or some by observing, etc.) and there are preferred mediums of learning for us to absorb the most for each of us and many of us have a preferred time in the day when we learn the most.

Hence, in the digital age, as we create the capability development agenda for organisations, some of the things we must be cognisant about are:

Learning Is Personal

How and what makes me learn the best has a strong bearing on me as a person. Hence look at the cross section of employees for whom the capability development agenda has been made, how they learn effectively, what makes them learn the most and design the curriculum accordingly. Dovetail the learning platforms accordingly to the overall agenda.

Capability Development Is an Organisational Priority

Various subunits in the ecosystem need to be broken down and then driven in terms of enabling the same. It's a business need, and hence a macro approach towards building capability within each subset needs to be firmed up keeping in mind the subset of employees, their personalities, learnability of a particular topic and how they can learn together effectively. It needs to be a mix of macro approach of capabilities and to the possible extent of micro approach on learning styles, personalities, effective mediums, etc. The mix needs to be well thought through before implementation.

Personalised Approach towards Capability Development for Hi Po

Once the talent management framework has created the Hi Po for the organisation, it's important that a personalised 3E-based (experience, exposure, education) individual development plan is drawn up for each Hi Po, and this should be a complete personalised approach to learning on the basis of the available learning styles, personal preferences, and organisational tools.

TWENTY-FIVE

Managing Performance Is Not About Post-mortem; It Needs to Be Fed Forward

If you are working in the corporate world, how many times have you got inside a room full of people reviewing the year gone by, the month gone by, the week gone by, etc., with large decks of beautifully crafted presentations and drawing lessons from the past. The answer will be innumerable times. There lies one of the biggest challenges of the corporate world. Our infatuation to learn from the past, look at the rear-view mirror is abnormally high. By no means I am discouraging reflections, discouraging learning from the past, all those are important and pertinent. The purpose of all review meetings is improving from what we have done, how we can do better. In this regard reflecting on what we have done and where all we have to do better is important. This needs to be a small part of the review conversation. The large part of any review mechanism for managing performance should be how we can ensure the future is better. The post-mortem of the past is good but it's just a learning and you cannot change the past. With the progress in the world of data science and technology the analytics of past performance is at our fingertip. We can always go through the analytics of the past and decipher important learning from it. To ensure a profitable future the leader needs to understand the levers for driving performance, the how of driving performance and review the how part much longer and in more rigorous manner.

If as leaders we review the 'how' part in greater detail instead of the 'what' part of the past, then we will actually enable the team to cross the bridge in a more effective way. The team would look at the leader as someone who empowers them and coaches them to drive performance rather than someone who only reviews the output post the month and provides expert comments. This kind of approach also encourages more transparent work ethic in the team. The team would be more open to talk about the challenges, problems, support required, etc., as they see the leader focussing on the how part and keen to help them cross the bridge. In post-mortem reviews, the team goes back into a shell and builds a strong defence mechanism of reasons, often keeping things under the carpet till it starts to show up in an ugly way. This does not happen in the case of reviews focused on the *how* part and of meetings on levers of performance. For the leader, thus, reviewing the *how* is all about steering the ship along with her army and guiding them to pull the right levers to steer the ship to the shore.

To ensure a review with large part of the meeting on discussing the *how* part, it's important that leaders are able to clearly pen down lead and lag indicators of performance in their respective business. While the outcome may be sales of certain the amount of units or profit of certain amount of money, it's important to define the levers of performance. Some of the common levers of performance in any business are the launch of products, launch of variants, cost-saving measures, supply-chain innovations, new product introductions, generating more cash, reduction of working capital, driving productivity, creating new business, paring of debts. It's important that the leader defines these levers well in the beginning of the year, and once firmed up, review them and build milestones for the team around these levers. The more the leader does this, the more she is chasing lead indicators and the more the leader is feeding forward the team. It's important to provide feedback but what engages and enable the team to deliver is feedforward. As the saying goes, 'Post-mortems are for the dead; to be alive and kicking, you got to feedforward and look ahead.'

TWENTY-SIX

Two Axiomatic Phrases towards Higher Organisation Effectiveness

Organisation effectiveness is an unending quest that every organisation must immerse themselves in in order to ensure continuous refinement of organisational outcomes. In a world of constant disruptions and never-ending change, constantly evaluating organisation effectiveness is more relevant today than ever before. This chapter reflects on two phrases that can help us plan our strategy towards ensuring higher organisation effectiveness.

Skin in the Game

The phrase refers to the book by N.N. Taleb[2] and many of the next set of to do things mentioned does have relevance to the book. In an organisation it is important that we are able to ensure that everyone in the organisation has skin in the game and none are advisers or consultants or are like them for whom there is no impact if the organisation wins

---

[2] Although the phrase refers to the book, it's origins are seen in horse derby races. It is usually attributed to Warren Buffett who initially invested in his own investment fund.

or loses. The risks in the organisation need to be shared. To ensure that everyone in the organisation has their skin in the game, it's important to ensure that accountabilities for each and every one is clearly defined. Everyone in the organisation, be it in the line function or support function, should have their targets aligned with the overall business unit targets. This is possible only through a robust performance planning mechanism in which not only the strategic objectives but the levers to the strategic objectives are clearly defined for all stakeholders till the last level in the organisation. The sales & commercial and manufacturing functions will always have their skin in the game as their objectives are directly related to the organisational objectives. It's important that functions such as operations, human resources, finance, shared services, corporate functions, etc., which are directly enabling the outcomes of commercial or manufacturing functions, have their KPI planned. Another key aspect that helps to drive accountability across the organisation in a more effective manner is the structuring of the organisation. The organisation structure should clearly align people with business objectives irrespective of the function they are working in. An organisation structure, if designed well, enables much higher accountability across the organisation.

Man in the Arena

This is a phrase which had become famous post the speech by Theodore Roosevelt on 23 April 1910. The phrase refers to giving credit to the person who it sweats out day in and day out under tremendous pressure and tries his level best with a positive attitude and lot of enthusiasm towards a given goal. The choice of the phrase has been done to emphasise on the fact that to enable an effective organisation there should be a tremendous focus on frontline workforce of the organisation be it the one who is selling or the one who is manufacturing. There should be a frontline obsession. If things in the organisation are made simpler for the frontline and they are able to spend more time in meeting the demands of the customers, then the outcome of the organisation is much more superior. To enable this in an organisation, it's important to look at aspects of empowerment of the frontline. For empowering the frontline, the decision matrix needs to be evaluated and it should always push down the decisions which are not high on impact instead of creating a bureaucratic blockage for the frontline. The other aspect of an organisation framework that helps to create a frontline obsession is communication. Strategic communication ensures that the impact of your message is consistent with your intentions, and results in understanding. What you say, the way you say it, where, when, and under what circumstances it is said shape the performance culture. To ensure higher organisation effectiveness it's important to evaluate the channels of communication of the leadership with the frontline workforce. How the leaders are able to make the frontline workforce understand the objectives and how they are able to motivate them towards a superior outcome through their communication channel is another important aspect.

TWENTY-SEVEN

Performance Culture: What Is It All About and Did You Notice It?

Organisation culture is the shared set of values, beliefs, and motives that guide behaviour in an organisation, the leaders demonstrate the behaviours guided by the values, beliefs, and motives at all times and over a period of time the culture of the organisation is built. Owing to the change in market and business context if there is a need to change the values, motives, and beliefs then there is a need to change the behaviours demonstrated and thereby the cultures. Organisation cultures evolve over a period of time due to economic, social, and business contexts, although it may not be drastically different however at times it can be significantly different to ensure sustainability. One of the top thought leaders on culture, Dr Edgar Schein, said in one of the interviews, '*Culture is what a group learns as its way of surviving and both getting along internally and solving its problems externally. What's usually missing is understanding how the external environment influences culture.*'

A performance culture is an attribute of an organisational culture, which implies performance orientation across the organisation for sustained business deliverables. It's a term which is used often by the CXO's to address their teams and in various conversations with stakeholders to signify better performance orientation. Performance culture is much broader than mere performance orientations. Lets reflect on its attributes and how it is visible to everyone and it's important. We reflect on visibility because there are a lot of visible and invisible elements of culture, and unlike the physical attributes of culture, which are readily visible, it's difficult to notice the invisible elements of culture, and hence have reflected on the attributes and the possible visible resultant elements of performance culture. The attributes of a performance culture are:

- High level of accountability: The focus of the organisation is delivering its promises to stakeholders.
- Customer-centric approach: Every move the organisation makes is with an eye on customers' needs and how best to serve the customers.
- Innovation oriented: Creating continuous disruptions in the marketplace and how to innovate to stay ahead of the curve with respect to competition.
- Highly agile mindset: Adaptive to change in the way business is run and to adapt to the changing marketplace.

In the world of business, it's the results which matter and it's important to note the resultant impact that gets created due to the performance culture in an organisation which can be easily observed. Also, to drive any culture it's important to focus on the visible elements of it and it's often very difficult to identify the visible elements which are not physical in nature. A high-performance culture is there if:

- The organisation is able to attract the best. The best in the industry would want to work in it.
- There is high level of pride in the organisation amongst its employees and thereby strong level of engagement.
- The organisation is able to continuously beat the competition and stay ahead of the curve in market share and profitability.
- All stakeholders and partners in the business value chain of the organisation want to associate and partner with the organisation.

TWENTY-EIGHT

Can Do Is Potential, *Will Do* Is Succession, and *Done It* Is Performance

Whenever we discuss talent in organisations or have people reviews for any business unit, the discussion is always around high potential talent—do we have the right mechanism to identify and develop them—then we discuss critical positions in the organisation and succession plans around it to ensure we keep the organisation derisked of potential talent shortages. I have been part of innumerable such discussions in my career as talent manager across organisations and across industries. When I reflect back on such discussions and then look back at some of the talents we discussed in these meetings and how their careers have shaped, the outliers, both in the positive and negative ranges of our assessment, are what amazes me the most. The size of these outliers is definitely small otherwise many of us would not have been in business. However it's important to reflect back on these outliers and how a few have managed to be considerably better than we assessed at a given point of time and a set of few have managed to not match up to the expectations than we thought they would, a closer look at their careers, their choices of roles and what led them to be outliers, I have arrived at the following aspects every talent who has been identified as high potential need to watch out for and these are also the aspects that organisations while continuously harnessing talent must imbibe in them to ensure the size of the outliers on the negative side of the talent assessment exercise is minimal.

Humility

Once a high potential (Hi Po) talent is identified and communicated about the same, there is a tendency to develop a bit of arrogance and know-it-all attitude due to adulation received from the organisation. It's important to stay humble amidst the adulation as otherwise it may create roadblocks for the talent to get things done and thus the performance outcomes since corporate jobs are team sport, amidst the matrixed way of working it's important to be humble and work together with the teams to get things done. At the end of the day its performance that counts. Talent managers continually need to provide continue and consider insight to talent on the interpersonal effectiveness of the talent in the organisation.

Curiosity

Often, talent in organisations get into their comfort zones and get into the know-it-all syndrome. Little do they realise after few years that what seemed like a great career has hit a roadblock as he or she has not focussed on learning and staying curious. Hence, it's important to do different things in an organisation or different organisations, continuously perform in each role and thus ensure being curious and thereby great learning all the time. Organisations that create great talent always focus on rotating talent across roles and continually challenging them to move into the next orbit.

Priority
The most difficult aspect to manage as talent moves on from being manager to manager's manager, is the ability to prioritise. It's not only about the job. The talent needs to prioritise effectively in work life and personal life and also amongst the two. The focus on managing work priorities, personal life priorities including health priorities is important as being unable to do so can be a huge roadblock for the talent to grow be it due to stress levels at work, broken relationships at home or bad health of self. For continued success it's important for talent to manage time effectively between his or her priorities. Organisations need to enable talent with a coach or mentor who is able to provide perspectives to talent and help them to prioritise.

Can-do Spirit
Many times, in various walks of life we have seen ordinary people achieving extraordinary results, the achievers may not have been extremely talented like many others in their arena, but they have achieved much higher than the talented ones. It's only because of the can-do attitude. At the end of the day in any organisation, it's the performance that counts, someone with high energy and can-do

attitude will always perform the best. It's important for the identified talents to continue have the can-do spirit as the high potential talent identification is not for ever. If the identification is not backed by continued high performance, it's a matter of time before which the talent hits a roadblock.

TWENTY-NINE

The Office Is Dead, Long Live the Office

As we encountered the lockdown for the first time in our lifetime and as we started to find a way to carry on with our lives and livelihood, we realised new ways of working around things which was an absolute not possible or we knew but doesn't work here phenomenon a few weeks before. Of the various memes that were floating around during the lockdown, the one that captured my imagination the most for its relevance was the one on how the pandemic was the reason for digital revolution of our workplaces and not any CXO.

Indeed, the pandemic leapfrogged our journey as organisations and as employees into the digital world. We learnt to do business digitally in all aspects of the business wherever it was possible. As we had no option but to change, we undertook the painful journey in our own small way with each one of us having a different set of problems to deal with the change. Due to the prolonged lockdown, the painful change slowly started to become a forced habit and being human, habits, become more comfortable than anything else as it's familiar to us. What was change management a few months back became the new normal.

As we got used to and became comfortable with the new normal slowly things turned back, and the country and economy started opening up. Offices started opening although with caution and limited days in a week, we were supposed to go to office. The same employees who had huge challenges in working from home once started talking about higher productivity in working from home and how beneficial it is for both the employee and the organisation. There were many who still wanted to go back to office and there were many who wanted to continue to work from home. However, one thing every office-goer agreed and truly started believing that there is no need to be in office every day and to get the work done for employees who work out of offices it's not necessary to be in the four walls called office contrary to what we all believed few months back. This insight was picked up by organisations across and each organisation depending on the industry started working towards leveraging on the work from home phenomenon for greater good of the organisation and employee both and started working on how they would want to evolve in the days ahead.

Did a benchmarking of few organisations across industries and found out that organisations are essentially looking at four broad themes to institutionalise the work from home culture in the days ahead:

- Define the roles that can work intermittently and roles which can work from home on continuous basis from home to ensure that business objectives are met at all times.

- Design and define the benefits and allowances to be provided in case of work from home to make the employee comfortable into the new way of life.
- Evaluate the infrastructure requirements in the changed scenario and how the organisation can reduce its fixed costs. This is to ensure that organisation derives the cost advantage.
- Define the guidelines on etiquettes for the new normal with both work from home and work from office scenarios coexisting in the workplace. This is to ensure work–life balance for employees.

Based on above parameters, organisations have worked on various models of work from home, be it complete work from home or a hybrid option, as it suits their industries. Every organisation is weighing its options and taking steps in this direction given the fluidity of the situation during the pandemic. The jury is still not out on this and will take some time to evolve. However, one thing is common: organisations are realising that social capital and work culture required when working from home may not be the same as when working from office. Therefore, it may not be possible to pick one over the other. In such a scenario, a hybrid culture is probably the way to go. Whatever be the verdict based on the situation at hand, organisations have to find the best option for business and its employees. It's certain that offices of tomorrow will not be the same as today's. Tomorrow's offices will be much different from what we are experiencing today and believed all our lives.

We have now realised the following in the digital world:
- That work can happen from anywhere; four walls of office do not define the boundary to work.
- It's far more productive to use the commuting time on working on an assignment for both the employee and the organisation.
- It's important to connect with colleagues and intermittent meetings in person along with being connected through telephone and internet can enable great work relationships as well.
- Flexibility in working hours creates better work life balance for the individual and enables better productivity for the organisation.
- Huge infrastructure to create offices is waste of resource for the organisation and offices can become much smaller in the days ahead.

To sum it up, as we traverse through the time and see our workplaces evolve taking the learnings of the pandemic and further evolve based on how our world shapes in the days ahead as the pandemic will continue for some time, it's for certain that the workplace we used to spend most of our time together and called it as office will definitely not be the same anymore. We may still call it office, but it will be much different in character, size, and demographics from what it exists today. The experiences we have of our offices will become history and we will live to tell tales of how offices used to be in the pre-pandemic era and how it changed forever in our lifetime.

THIRTY

Three Simple Steps to Effective Talent-Development Strategy

Organisations develop talent to ensure that the business deliverables are fulfilled through delighting customers and making the organisation future ready in terms of capability to withstand the disruptions in the market, economy, business lever, or the socio-political scenario.

Contrary to the belief of many managers that on-going talent-development initiatives help to engage and motivate talent, in reality, talent development is a serious business investment to generate greater profit like all investments are intended to do. The investments in talent development enable the organisation to plug the capability gaps to deliver the customer needs in the short run and build an ability within the organisation to navigate the unchartered future course with aplomb. If the investments are not done on time then organisations pay a heavy price by bringing in external experts who charge the organisation a phenomenal amount to fix the capability gaps to deliver as per customer needs or the organisation need to hire external talent at much higher price thus increasing manpower costs and disturbing the internal parity both. In certain cases, the solution is a mix of both as well.

Like in the case of all investments, it's important to know the levers that produce the best returns and accordingly optimise those levers. For talent development, there are only three levers that any organisation's talent-development strategy should focus on. The *first lever* is about focusing on managerial capability development; the *second lever* is on strengthening the overall capability of the teams either at a functional level or at a business level; and the *third lever* is on top talent development to strengthen the succession pipeline.

Let's reflect a bit more on these three levers that ensure an effective talent-development strategy.

Managerial Capability Development

Organisations with clearly articulated value systems and competency levels should focus on developing managers behaviourally more aligned to the value systems of the organisation and functionally more aligned to the functional competency levels. Talent-development initiatives should just focus on these two areas for managers and constantly train, assess, and develop them on this. With the changing market and business environment the organisations leadership must relook at the values and the functional competencies defined, but once it is defined, the talent-development teams should just focus on building a great value system and high levels of functional competencies in managers. If managers are developed on the value system of the organisation and have great functional competence, then they propagate the same in their teams and across the organisation, and eventually the organisation is able to emerge stronger in the marketplace.

Overall Capability of Teams

Apart from managers, the other focus area for talent development should be to fulfil the capability gaps of the teams be it the functional teams or business teams. The talent-development team should discuss with the leadership in various functional and business areas, identify top three capability gaps in their function or business, and focus their efforts on those three capability gaps. A clear road map to develop a framework to assess the development and a timeline to complete the journey is all that is needed to make it happen.

Top Talent Development

Top talent development is the third lever, which should be a part of an organisation's talent-development strategy as it enables the organisation to develop a robust succession mechanism and enough bench strength for its future growth. Talent development in this case is a focused approach of development basis the gap in individual's ability and the requirement in the job which he or she has been identified as the successor. The process for identification of top talent and key roles they require need to be championed by the business leadership and HR leadership together to enable the talent-development team to effectively execute the development agenda around top talent development.

THIRTY-ONE

Tough Times Never Last but Tough People Do

Almost 4 months into the COVID-19 pandemic, the first lockdown hit India. The next 4 months were such a disastrous experience for all of us. Every one of us has a different story to tell on how we coped with the change and how it affected our lives. We are still grappling with the unprecedented challenges it brought in our lives.

When the pandemic started, we saw organisations executing their business continuity plans, forming core teams to manage the health and safety of their employees at a unit and corporation levels, creating greater levels of engagement with the teams by the leaders. Many organisations created teams to learn and understand the best practices of other countries, and imbibed the leanings in the Indian context to stay ahead of the race. We did all these initially with the hope that post lockdown the curve will come down and things will go back to being normal again. To deal with the situation, we saw a few managers putting their favourite talents in the core teams to make them heroes in the near term.

However, the reality was way different than anticipated. We heard about community spread raging through the population and knew that the pandemic will stay until a vaccine was found. Many of us, our colleagues, friends, and relatives, were infected. Managers who had installed their favourite talents in important positions were now relying on the not-so-favourite ones as the reality sank in and they became aware that it was going to be long-drawn challenges with not much reward at the end. The pandemic was going to be a part of our lives for some time. We could only hope we remain safe.

With gloom all around, it was natural to be mentally affected and to feel low. It was absolutely normal to feel emotionally drained at times. However, this cannot be something that dictated our feelings, taking control of our lives. It was important for all of us to realise that this was a phase in our lives, and if we were able to overcome it successfully, we were going emerge stronger and better. There needed to be a sense of optimism built in all of us on the road ahead and loads of courage to battle the unknown. The more we were able to tap into a positive mindset, the more we were able to adapt to the new way of life, to conform to the new daily work management principles, to find happiness in small things in life, and were better able to overcome the challenges on that hit us. Today, as we look back on those difficult days, let's all cheer up with the thought 'tough times never last but tough people do' and stay positive for the great things that await us in life.

THIRTY-TWO

Why Did You Take HR?

Last week, I conducted a session for the new HR batch in a very reputed B-school. As a part of the introductory talk, I asked the students the dreaded question 'Why did you take HR?' This question is often thrown at HR students up until their early careers. Like me and many of my batchmates, they gave the usual reply: 'I like to work with people,' 'I am a people person, and so I thought I will thrive in HR,' and a few other similar ones. After years of experience and exposure in the business world and in the domain of human resource, I realised how naive we were as students in understanding about the choice we made and how much far away from reality was our understanding of the ingredients of a successful HR leader.

The career choices we make in India are more often driven by the need to get a good job and a steady income in the long run rather than in the interest or understanding of what it takes to pursue a certain field of education. I would not want to generalise this for everyone in India and would rather say it is true for many like me who come from certain background and certain social system.

With the exposure and experience of HR today, the dreaded question is not *so* dreaded anymore. The choices

I made, although with a faint understanding of HR, were indeed good choices. Given the learnings for over decades now, let me share my thoughts on what is required to be able to effectively manage human resources. Based on your interests and likes, the insights I'm going to share here will enable you to take a more informed decision on whether you should consider HR as a career option.

To be an effective human resource manager, the following traits are necessary:

Understanding How People Think and Act Differently as Individuals and in Teams

To enable this understanding, it's important to have an in-depth understanding of human psychology and organisation behaviour. It's important to learn how people get motivated, how they behave in teams, how conflicts can be resolved constructively, and how people can be reinforced positively and negatively to condition behaviours.

Thoroughly Understand the Various Processes and Systems

It is vital to not just understand but thoroughly so the processes and systems in your organisation to be able to effectively asses, develop, and reinforce human behaviours. You need tools to manage and drive behaviours needed to run business effectively. These can be found by answering the questions how to build a performance management system, how to reward, how to define and develop competencies, how to train different types of individuals effectively, etc.—essentially, a deep understanding of the tool kit to manage and develop human resources. This includes understanding of labour laws and labour relations.

An In-depth Business Understanding and the Ability to Proffer HR Solutions to Business Problems

This is a very important trait, which is imbibed more through experience and exposure to various business set-ups and situations. The learning is more thorough if the contexts of businesses are different. To develop this, it's important to understand the dimensions of doing business, such as costs, finances, operational efficiency measures, investment horizons, business drivers, and the overall strategy. Unless the HR professional is able to derive business value for the stakeholder, the efforts will never count; hence, a thorough business understanding will equip the HR professional to think through a solution by keeping the business interest in mind.

THIRTY-THREE

Attributes That Make a Leader

Leadership is one of the most important and invested topic within organisational boards and governance committees as well as among businesspersons. It is so because quality leadership has the potential to catapult an ordinary business into an extraordinary one. Good leadership can transform an ordinary performer into an extraordinary one. Therefore, creating a succession pipeline of excellent leadership is one of the core responsibilities of boards and CXOs in an organisation. Each organisation, on the basis of winning competencies required to drive its business outcomes, creates a leadership model and drives the assessment development and deployment of the leadership pipeline thus created.

While organisations will continue to create templates and update their leadership requirement models to reaffirm the pipeline in a certain way, there are certain aspects of leadership that are transient across leadership models, subcultures, and organisations. Before we understand those aspects of leadership, let's take a look at what it means to be a leader beyond designations, definitions, and positions.

Often when managers assume large roles with the ability to impact their organisations and people, they begin to think of themselves as leaders. As a consequence of which organisations refer to them as leaders. However, in reality, they may be just managers and not leaders. If you have no followers, no one idolises you, no one really wants to emulate you, and no one wants to be like you, are you then really a leader or just an efficient manager? Leading a large team does not necessarily make someone a leader. Leaders have followers—a large numbers—who wants to emulate them for who they are. A leader is someone who inspires others to do more and grow more.

With a bit more understanding of what a leader should be, isn't it clear that the attributes of a true leader are similar across the value chain and geographies? And it seems that the attributes are much more than the leadership model of an organisation.

The attributes that really enable leaders to stand out are authenticity, humility, and magnanimity. These are a must have for a great leader. While each of these three are topics to be discussed and discovered in themselves, a lot has been written about them. Of the three, though, I want to particularly double click on 'magnanimity', which is not as much written about, unlike the other two, but is an equally important attribute of a leader. Being magnanimous is to be generous and forgiving. In the cutthroat world of business, where everyone is looking for more opportunity and profit, it's the secure leader with immense self-confidence and high level of competence who is magnanimous. This magnanimity is not only displayed at the team level but also at the peer level. It's definitely one of the most difficult leadership attributes to imbibe. Leaders evolve and learn to be magnanimous over time; it doesn't happen in a day. Leaders who have reached the level where they are continually demonstrating magnanimity, authenticity, and humility are the ones who have arrived. They have made sure that their legacies will outlive them in their fields of work and in the minds and hearts of the people they work with.

About the Author

Biswaroop Mukherjee is an experienced HR leader. He has handled multiple high-impact roles in the domain of HR in various organisations of repute across industries and geographies. Biswaroop's journey in HR began with a passion for understanding the intricacies of human behaviour in the workplace and a drive to create positive organisational cultures that foster growth and development. His interests and expertise are wide ranging, encompassing such eclectic fields as organisation development, change management, executive coaching, and building high-performing teams.

Biswaroop completed his management education from SIBM, Pune, and bachelor's in science from Fergusson College, Pune. He has been associated with Tata Motors for over a decade now and is currently employed as the HR head of the Commercial Vehicle Business Unit. Biswaroop has handled various roles at Tata Motors prior to his current role. He has also worked at reputed organisations such as GE, Deloitte, Dr. Reddy's, and ABP Group in the past.

An ICF-certified coach and a Hogan-certified assessor, he has developed a keen interest in human resource development and management. His diverse background equips him with a unique perspective on the challenges and opportunities facing HR practitioners in today's fast-paced and ever-changing business environment. Driven by a commitment to continuous learning and professional development, Biswaroop has earned certifications in executive coaching and assessment and regularly participates in industry conferences and workshops.

www.ingramcontent.com/pod-product-compliance
Lightning Source LLC
LaVergne TN
LVHW041853070526
838199LV00045BB/1585